BLESSED JERZY POPIEŁUSZKO

BERNARD BRIEN

Blessed Jerzy Popiełuszko

Truth versus Totalitarianism

With the collaboration of
Charles Wright

Translated by Michael J. Miller

IGNATIUS PRESS   SAN FRANCISCO

Original French edition:
Jerzy Popiełuszko: La vérité contre la totalitarisme
© 2016, Groupe Artège
Editions Artège, 9, espace Méditerranée; 66000 Perpignan, France

Cover art:
Jerzy Popiełuszko (1947–1984)
Image based on a photograph by an anonymous photographer
Wikimedia Commons Image

Cover design by Enrique J. Aguilar

To Loïc and Nicolas

How unsearchable are his judgments
and how inscrutable his ways!

—Romans 11:33

Blessed are those who are persecuted
    for righteousness' sake,
for theirs is the kingdom of heaven.

—Matthew 5:10

Contents

Preface

I was the bishop of Luçon when I met Bernard for the first time at the request of the director of the diocesan vocation office. He lived then in Les Sables-d'Olonne, was approaching the age of sixty, and was working in commerce. With his characteristic volubility, he told me about his encounter with Christ in a seaside chapel run by the Community of the Beatitudes, then about the call to become a priest that had rung in his ears shortly after this decisive spiritual experience. Rather quickly I perceived the authenticity of his conversion, the depth of his call. Of course, as a candidate for the priesthood, he had an unconventional background—he had been married twice, was the father of two sons and a grandfather several times over. Nevertheless, I sensed interiorly that it was necessary to take him seriously, that his desire was not a whim but had something to do with the Spirit of God. After consulting with several canonists who all confirmed for me the absence of any impediment to his ordination, I decided to form a little team to accompany him on his journey. I wanted to give him every opportunity to succeed and, at the same time, to determine whether his vocation would withstand the test of time. As the months went by, reports from the ground confirmed my intuition: Bernard demonstrated abilities that substantiated the sincerity of his response. It was not an insignificant thing to go back to being a student at his age, to agree to live a communal life in a rectory, to take on volunteer work among the poor and the hospitalized. Bernard accepted all that very humbly, without ever complaining or showing impatience. I had to acknowledge that the months passed by, but his vocation to the priesthood did not pass away.

When I became the bishop of Créteil in 2007, Bernard asked me whether I could accept him into my diocese to complete his formation. I had detected in him a charism for accompanying the sick, and more generally all fragile persons, toward whom he showed a wealth of compassion. Furthermore, he had an innate sense of personal contact and of listening and, like all converts, a great desire to help as many people as possible to discover the face of Christ. This is why, after his ordination on April 15, 2012, I appointed him assistant priest in a parish of the diocese, while entrusting to him the responsibility of being the priest chaplain of the local hospitals. Right in Chenevier Hospital in Créteil, through the mediation of Bernard, who had come to administer the Anointing of the Sick to a dying patient, a miracle took place through the intercession of Blessed Jerzy Popiełuszko, as described at the beginning of this book. God willing, this "miracle of Créteil" will enable the chaplain of Solidarność, the martyr of Communism, to be raised to the honor of the altars as a saint.

In September 2014, while I was starting the diocesan investigation for the canonization process during a Mass celebrated in the monastery of the Sisters of the Annonciade, in Thiais, this memory occurred to me: in 2011, during a pilgrimage to Poland, as I was meditating at his tomb, I entrusted the governance of my diocese to the prayers of Blessed Jerzy. I think, therefore, that through this miracle, although God visited Poland, he also visited the Marne Valley region. In my view there is a clear sign here of the Lord's passage in the life of our diocese. We must accept this sign humbly, in faith, knowing that we are always too insignificant for such a grace.

This preface is rightly an occasion to give thanks for the faith journey of Father Bernard. His vocation has sometimes caused misunderstandings and resistance. And yet, through this priest with the atypical résumé, the Lord has shown his mercy by working this cure. I want to give thanks also for Father Jerzy Popiełuszko, whose life, dedicated to the service of truth, is recounted in this book. May this volume strengthen a little more the already very deep ties that unite the Diocese of Créteil and Poland!

—Bishop Michel Santier

The French Miracle

The most incredible thing about
miracles is that they happen.

— Gilbert Keith Chesterton

July 2012. With Hubert, a religious friend, I was criss-crossing Poland in the footsteps of John Paul II. I had just been ordained a priest several weeks before, at the canonical age of . . . sixty-five years. In clerical language, that is called a "late vocation". I must admit that, where faith was concerned, I have never been very precocious. After spending the greater part of my life far from the Church, I made up again with God at the age of fifty-seven. It happened one day in May 2004. My second marriage was on the rocks. I was desperate because of this new failure that confirmed the collapse of my life. That day, prompted by I know not what inspiration, I went through the door of a little chapel in Les Sables-d'Olonne, at the seashore. It had been ages since I had gone into a church. As soon as I crossed the threshold, I felt that I was seized, enveloped by a presence. I remained there for more than an hour, in silence, awkwardly starting a dialogue with God that resembled a prayer. As I left the chapel, with my heart calmed and at the same time inflamed, I knew that now nothing would be as it had been before. In fact, several months after that conversion, I heard a call to the priesthood. After testing the truth of it, my bishop confirmed my vocation. I then set out on a long journey of formation, with plenty of obstacles, but concluding with my ordination at the cathedral in Créteil on April 15, 2012.[1] In order to celebrate this entrance into the priesthood, I treated myself to this tour of Poland as a present.

Before visiting the Marian shrine of Częstochowa, Hubert had suggested a stop in a suburb of Warsaw. "I would like to show you the parish of Saint Stanisłaus Kostka where Father Jerzy Popiełuszko is buried", he said. I had never heard anything about the place, and the name of the priest meant nothing to me. I found myself entering the church with the two towers standing proudly against the sky. There was nothing special about it, but I thought that it was prayerful, and I felt at ease in it. Around the choir I noticed a whole series of panels depicting the life of Blessed Jerzy, the former assistant pastor of the parish. I discovered that this Polish priest with the gentle, youthful face had been the chaplain of the labor union Solidarność, founded by Lech Wałęsa, that he was considered the symbol of a whole population's spiritual resistance against Communism, that he had been killed by the police of the regime in 1984, at the age of thirty-seven, and that his ardent commitment to the truth, sealed by his martyrdom, had melted the ice of totalitarianism. Finally, on a plaque recording details about his life, I discovered that he was born on September 14, 1947, exactly the same day as I! What could have been a mere detail made a very

---

[1] I describe this journey at greater length in the epilogue of this book, pp. 111ff.

vivid impression on me and immediately made the priest close and familiar to me, as though these coincidental births had formed between us an invisible tie, a sort of twinning.

Upon my return to France, I purchased all the books that had been published on the subject. I had a great thirst for knowledge. I wanted to understand his life, his context, his impact. I informed myself compulsively, spending hours on the internet, asking the help of Polish friends. Jerzy was no longer just an object of knowledge: an intimate relationship had formed between us. Every day, after Morning Prayer, I recited the prayer of thanksgiving for his canonization. I increasingly felt that he was present at my side. Within a few weeks, he had become a companion, a friend, a brother.

Friday, September 14, 2012, scarcely two months after my trip to Poland. I am calmly finishing lunch in the sun-drenched yard of the rectory. At around three o'clock in the afternoon, my cell phone vibrates in my pocket. I recognize the voice of the caller, Sister Rozalia, who coordinates the chaplaincy at Chenevier Hospital in Créteil. She asks me to come for an emergency visit to a dying patient. I arrive in the patient's room at about 3:30. The room is spotlessly clean, white, somewhat cold, the sort that you find in all hospitals; in the middle of it, stretched out on a bed, lies an unconscious man in a comatose state, in the terminal phase. I meet his wife, Chantal, who sketches a portrait of him for me. Fifty-six years old, the father of three daughters, a consultant in a property law firm, a fervent Christian, François has battled for eleven years with a blood cancer, an extremely rare form of leukemia called atypical myeloproliferative disease. For two months his condition has been deteriorating. The descent has been breathtaking: despite three chemotherapies and a bone marrow graft, the cancer cells have spread throughout his body. "The cancer is everywhere", Chantal insists, before continuing, her voice choked with emotion: "Last August the doctors warned me that there was nothing else to do, except palliative treatments while waiting for the inevitable outcome. In September, François left Henri-Mondor Hospital, where he had been treated from the beginning, to come to this hospital, which specializes in palliative care, and to prepare to die." In our conversation, I learn that she has scheduled an appointment with the funeral home to plan the burial . . .

On the dying man's bedside table I place a candle, the cross of John Paul II, the holy chrism, and a picture of Father Jerzy Popiełuszko that has not left me since my trip to Poland. Then, flanked by Rozalia and Chantal, I administer to François the sacrament of the sick. I recall an intense moment of very deep prayer. After completing the sacramental rite, I realize that it is September 14, the day of our common birthday—Father Popiełuszko's and mine. I spontaneously suggest to Chantal that she entrust François to the intercession of the Blessed and that we recite together the prayer for his canonization. At the end of the prayer, I turn interiorly to the Polish priest, and, as one friend speaks to another, I murmur to him these few words: "Listen, Jerzy, today is September 14, your birthday and mine, and so if you are supposed to do something for our brother François, this is the day!" Shortly after that, Sister Rozalia and I make ourselves scarce, convinced that we have said adieu to François.

The next day, a telephone call from Rozalia surprises me around noon: "Father Bernard, Father Bernard, it is unbelievable!" she says in a voice that betrays great excitement. "I just returned from François' room. I thought that he had died, but he was sitting up, showered, and shaved. It is a miracle, Father Bernard, it is a miracle!"

I owe to Chantal, the only witness, the account of what happened the day before after I left: "As soon as you had left his room, François opened his eyes, smiled, and asked what had happened. I had the impression that a veil was being torn, that my husband, like Lazarus, was emerging from the tomb. For the first time in weeks he spoke words coherently, with a normal diction. And during the night, despite the intravenous fluids and catheters, he managed to get up three times to walk as far as the bathroom door!"

The following days only confirm the evidence: François is doing well! Moreover he goes back home as of late September. All the medical tests that follow one after the other converge on this diagnosis: complete remission of the disease! The doctors are astounded. Whereas scans only a few days ago revealed the attacks of the disease on the bones, today the cancerous cells have completely disappeared. François is cured. "After an in-depth examination, I certify that his rapid cure, starting on September 14, 2012, when he was in palliative care, has no medical explanation", declares Doctor Jean-Michel Dormont, the physician treating François, in a signed certificate dated December 7, 2012. One and a half years later, in March 2014, it is the turn of Professor Catherine Cordonnier, head of the clinical hematology and cellular therapy department of Henri-Mondor Hospital, who has treated François from the start, to confirm the total remission of the disease. I still see her in her great white coat, at the end of a corridor in the hospital, admit to me somewhat disconcertedly, "It is a spectacular, or rather, miraculous case!"

I let some time pass before telling my ordinary, Bishop Michel Santier. Deep down, I knew that this was a miracle, a miracle due to the intercession of Father Popiełuszko. It seemed interiorly self-evident. But I felt also that it was necessary to keep silence. In order for a miracle to be recognized, the cure must be spontaneous and total, which was the case, but it must also be confirmed over time. So patience was required.

Therefore I kept this secret for almost seven months. Seven long months during which my relationship to Jerzy became deeper and even more intense, almost to the point of fusion. But the wait also plunged me into the depths of reflections. Unceasingly I asked myself: Why had the Lord chosen me, with my chaotic, tortuous career, to be the instrument of his grace? Were there not more exemplary, more respectable servants? Why did he make use of my hands to reveal his mercy and to save François? Was it—and I think this is the answer—to confirm me in my vocation as a priest, several months after my ordination? Haunted by these questions, I used to wake up in the middle of the night. Even today I do not understand it. I am still like a poor man with regard to all this. When God passes by, you feel very insignificant. The only thing to do is to imitate Mary, in other words, to kneel down and to marvel: "The Lord . . . has done great things for me, and holy is his name" (Lk 1:49).

After I informed my bishop, in May 2013, events moved faster. Monsignor Tomasz Kaczmarek, postulator of Father Jerzy's cause, came from Poland to meet us: François, Chantal, and me. Based on our discussions, he decided right away to accept the miracle to advance the Polish priest's cause of canonization. "Of all the cures attributed to the intercession of the Blessed, this is the clearest, the most evident", he said, immediately settling the matter. In September 2014, at the request of the Archbishop of Warsaw, Cardinal Nycz, Bishop Santier therefore opened the diocesan investigation of the canonization process, since the cure occurred in his Diocese of Créteil. After one year of work, the interrogation of all the witnesses, and the examination of the medical file, the investigatory commission acknowledged the authenticity of the miracle, thus opening the way to the canonization of Father Popiełuszko. This was on September 14, 2015, at the cathedral in Créteil. The dossier is now in Rome, in the hands of the Congregation for the Causes of Saints, which has to present it to Pope Francis. The final decision is up to him, whether to put his signature on the decree authorizing Jerzy to join the procession of the saints. With all my Polish friends I am holding my breath. I am confident!

In any case, how can we not marvel at this continuity? Three popes have looked into Jerzy's sanctity. In 1997, John Paul II opened his process of beatification. Benedict XVI beatified him in 2010, as a martyr of the faith. And, God willing, Francis will soon admit him to the honor of the altars, through the grace of this French miracle, of which I was the instrument, the "unworthy servant" of which the Gospel speaks (Lk 17:10).

In prayer I often ask the Lord why he let Jerzy barge into my life in this way: I knew nothing about his existence a few years ago, and today he is very present to me on a daily basis. Did he mean to propose him to me as a model for my priestly life, an example to follow, somewhat like the Curé of Ars, who had guided me as I was preparing for the priesthood? Was it so that I might make his life, his message, and his witness known—something that I feel urged to do?

As I write these lines, we are a few weeks away from the World Youth Day in Kraków, which will take place under the banner of mercy. These days are an opportunity to propose models of sanctity to young people, and Father Jerzy appears on the list of these patron saints to imitate and follow. I decided to write this book for them, to present to them the figure of this priest who changed the face of Poland and, incidentally, also transformed my life. Our world manufactures a constant stream of heroes, stars, and celebrities who are adulated one day and forgotten the next. It is important to offer for the admiration of young people something other than these spoiled examples from the entertainment world. May they hitch their dreams to more secure posts: these saints who will never be outmoded and are genuinely provocative, since they dared to risk their lives and to sow joy and peace! Father Popiełuszko is of that caliber. His life is a miracle, a gift from God, a fabulous embodiment of the Gospel. His whole life, marked with courage, truth, and justice, testifies that Jesus liberates and transforms human beings and cultures and that for him no cause is desperate. Father Jerzy and I are the witnesses to this: walking alongside him elevates life to a dizzying height and intensity! With all my heart I wish that everyone could experience this companionship which fulfills life.

1

A Slavic Youth

*I have called you by name,
you are mine.*

—Isaiah 43:1

Jerzy's story begins in Okopy, a remote hamlet in the northeast of traditional, Catholic Poland, in the voivodeship of Białystok, near the Russian border, where his family had been settled for generations. His parents, Władysław and Marianna Kalinowski, were simple farmers. They raised grains and some potatoes and also raised a regiment of poultry to vary the daily routine. In that corner of the wilderness, surrounded by immense forests, the climate is harsh and the soil poor. It takes a lot of drudgery to earn a living.

Born on September 14, 1947, the feast day of the Exaltation of the Holy Cross, Jerzy was the next-to-last of five children. He received Baptism in the little parish church in Suchowola, where he would memorize the answers from the catechism and sow the prayers of his childhood. Every day he traveled on foot the three miles between the church and the family home to attend morning Mass!

He seemed so frail, so weak that his father understood that he could not count on him to help with the chores.

In fact, the youngest brother, the robust Stanisław, eventually took over the farm.

From his parents, who were simple, pious people, Jerzy received a loving education and the homespun values that unfolded throughout his life: humility, dedication, industriousness, a sense of the effort, dignity, and love of his ancestors, whose memory must be honored, since one owes to them what one is. But the finest, most precious heritage that he received from his parents was the Gospel, the landmark of the years of his youth. Father Piotr Bożyk, who taught him catechism, remembers a young boy attracted to Christ as though magnetically drawn to the truth: "You had the impression that he wanted to swallow in one gulp all the degrees of holiness. The boy was religiously insatiable and appreciated the value of the interior life." [1]

One of his brothers relates that when he was eight or nine years old, Jerzy had made a sort of altar with a few scraps of wood and spent whole days playing at imitating the priest's gestures.

Did Jerzy's desire mature little by little, like a plant in the sunlight, or did he hear the call on a particular day? Was it while watching the parish priest during Mass, which he served as an altar boy, that he intuited that very important things were going on there around the altar? Did the passing of his sister Jadwigę, who died when she was two years old, affect the infancy of his vocation by opening a little window onto the invisible? In any case, at a very young age Jerzy sensed in the depths of his heart the call to become a priest. One day he announced it to

---

[1] All the quotations by witnesses or by Jerzy Popiełuszko himself that are printed without references are taken from the collection by Msgr. Ryszard Wasik, *Le père Jerzy Popieluszko: "Mon cri était celui de ma patrie": Témoignages* (Mareil-Marly: Aide à l'église en détresse [Aid to the Church in Need], 2008).

his parents. Władysław and Marianna accepted the news as a gift from God, with faith and thanksgiving.

At the secondary school in Suchowola, where he became a boarding student in 1961, Jerzy deepened his quest. He was a frail boy, timid but intense. He liked literature and Polish history, devoured the lives of the saints, especially that of Maximilian Kolbe, the Polish Franciscan who illumined the hell of Auschwitz with his faith, hope, and charity. To characterize his demand for truth, his friends called him the "philosopher".

When he reached the age of seventeen, the hour had come to leave his familiar surroundings and to make the great leap. With his diploma in his pocket, there he was en route to the capital. He could have opted for the seminary in his diocese, but he chose the one in Warsaw, where the rector was Cardinal Wyszyński, that great figure of resistance to the Sovietization of Poland, for whom Jerzy had fervent admiration.

In the midst of rebuilding, Warsaw still bore the scars of the war. The city was one big open-air construction site. Housed in a former Carmelite monastery, Saint John the Baptist Seminary resembled a barracks, and the rooms of the seminarians, situated along endless corridors, seemed like prison cells.

Having little natural aptitude for studies, Jerzy excelled neither in philosophy nor in theology, but he did distinguish himself by the rare qualities of his heart. "His own weaknesses, his repeated sicknesses had made him more keenly sensitive to the suffering of others", one of his professors, Father Wiesław Kądziela, recalls. "Jerzy spent his time caring for them; in the city there was always someone whom he visited and served. He saw his apostolate in very concrete terms, as they taught us then: we evangelize with deeds; words merely help."

At that time the seminarian appeared to be an ordinary young man, rather reserved but joyful, smiling, at ease with himself, even carefree, as shown by photos from those days in which Jerzy, surrounded by a group of friends, poses on skis at the top of the slopes. There was nothing distinctive about him, except perhaps an uncommon attention to others, a great sense of the spiritual outlook, and the contagious enthusiasm with which he looked forward to his future mission as a priest. He was glad about the liturgical reforms introduced by Vatican Council II: for him, Mass celebrated "facing the people" and the possible use of Polish now during the celebration were so many means of communicating with the faithful, the Polish Christians with whom he would soon celebrate a spiritual wedding.

Military service was a break in his itinerary. It was the end of the carefree days and the beginning of the sufferings.

It was October 1966, and Jerzy was not yet twenty years old. Several days after he received the cassock, he was called up to put on a uniform, like all the young men of his age, but with the special treatment that the Communist regime reserved for future priests.

You must recall that, since the end of World War II, Poland had been under the iron rule of the Soviet Union. Rebaptized the "Polish People's Republic" in 1952, the country was subject to dictatorship controlled by Moscow and based on the Marxist-Leninist ideology, which was very hostile to Christianity.

Jerzy was enlisted in Bartoszyce, in a special unit reserved for seminarians in which all sorts of stratagems were devised to break the young boys and to drive any idea of a vocation from their heads. All day long the trainers sang the siren song of the Marxist-Leninist catechism or else held out the prospect of girls and an easy life. Indoctrination, threats, bullying: they would try anything to make them repudiate their faith.

For two years, Jerzy endured that trial and put up with that constant harassment. "They try to break us with fatigue, they drive us relentlessly and hound me, but I am very tough; they will not ruin my vocation either by threats or by torture", he wrote to his parents.

One day an officer noticed a gleaming object around his neck: "Who is pictured on your medal?" he asked. "It is the Blessed Virgin, the Queen of Poland", calmly replied the seminarian, who had a great devotion to Mary. "Now you are going to trample on that for me, or I will pulverize you", the soldier threatened, pulling on the chain, which did not give way. Drawing his strength from the prayers of the Rosary, to which his mother had initiated him, and from the *Prison Notes* of Cardinal Wyszyński, who recommends enduring insults and injustices without ever responding to provocation, Jerzy refused to obey. He was severely beaten and thrown into solitary confinement for a month. It was his first act of resistance to authority. There would be others . . .

Jerzy Popiełuszko returned greatly weakened by those two years of military service. The demands, the persecutions left an indelible mark on his health.

At that same time, I for my part was employed as a salesman at the Comptoir Moderne, the ancestor of French supermarkets, in Le Mans. It was an adventurous, active life

into which I threw myself enthusiastically, determined
to climb all the rungs of success. I was a carefree baby-
boomer, an avid fan of soccer, which I almost made my
profession, and of automobiles. This is a big contrast with
Jerzy, who by then had started his path toward martyrdom and understood that there is a price for truth and fi-
delity to Christ. "True love is demanding; it requires sacrifices", he would later say, adding: "Truth, too, must cost
something. Truth that does not cost anything is a lie."[2]

---

[2] Jerzy Popiełuszko, "Homélie lors de la messe pour la patrie de mai 1984",
in Popiełuszko, *Le Chemin de ma croix: Messes à Varsovie* (Paris: Cana, 1984),
177.

2

Broken Hearts

*I am the good shepherd; I know my
own and my own know me.*

—John 10:14

May 28, 1972. A day of celebration at the Cathedral of
Saint John the Baptist in Warsaw, where thirty seminarians would soon become priests. Their procession passed
through the enormous red brick portal of the sanctuary.
With their long white albs and their boyish faces, one
would say that it was a procession of angels. In the middle
of that column which split the very large crowd that had
come to the ordination, one could make out the grace-
ful form of Jerzy. The young man was twenty-five years
old. His serious mien expressed profound recollection. As
he walked toward the altar to be presented to Cardinal
Wyszyński, the primate of Poland, who was presiding at
the liturgy, his glance met that of his beaming parents,
who were seated at the back of the cathedral.

During the very prayerful liturgy, which was marked
especially by the prostration of the ordinands during the
recitation of the litany of the saints, Jerzy walked toward
the cardinal. The latter placed on him the stole and the
chasuble and anointed the palms of his hands with sacred chrism. From then on he was a priest. It was a great

grace to receive the sacrament from the hands of the primate. For him and his compatriots, Cardinal Wyszyński
was much more than the leader of the Polish Church: he
represented the legitimacy of the nation. Moreover, the
esteem was mutual. The primate had spotted the young
man at the seminary and had taken him under his wing.
Impressed by the goodness and faith that streamed from
that frail youth, he considered him his spiritual son.

After his ordination, Father Jerzy "learned the ropes" in
several parishes in the vicinity of Warsaw: first in Ząbki,
a working-class suburb of the capital, then in Anin, until he joined the parish of the Infant Jesus in Żoliborz in
1978. There his health showed the first signs of fatigue.
Being anemic, Jerzy had been subject to frequent dizzy
spells since his military service. One day he fainted right in
the middle of Mass. This was followed by a serious hem-
orrhage that obliged him to spend weeks in the hospital,
where his stays became more and more frequent.

"God sends me to preach the Gospel and to bind up the
brokenhearted." This motto, printed on the commemora-
tive card distributed by Jerzy at his First Mass, nicely ex-
presses his way of carrying out his ministry: as a service
rendered to his parishioners, and especially to the poor-
est, to the least significant among them, who are exposed
to suffering, whom he wished to take into his apostolic
heart. There was something of the Curé of Ars in Father
Jerzy: the same vision of ministry as an "engagement" to
the faithful, the same love for the flock that was entrusted
to him, the same selfless commitment in soothing the people's pains, taking their burdens on his shoulders, the same
love for the Sacrament of Penance, the privileged place for
manifesting the mercy of the Father.

Although he recalls the figure of Saint John Vianney, Father Jerzy also resembles the priest Pope Francis says he wants to see: not the "custodian of sacred oil" shut away in the sacristy and in himself, but the pastor "who has the smell of the sheep" and is always going out to meet them, attentive to the reality of their daily lives, sharing their joys and sorrows, their fears and hopes.

Concerned about overcoming distance and putting himself at the level of the people, Father Popiełuszko opened his apartment to the four winds. He was ceaselessly visiting the homes of the faithful, conversing about their work, about the concerns of their family, about the health of each one. The man had a gift for encounter, relationship, friendship. His mere presence brought about communion. Father Józef Maj, who was at seminary with him, recalls: "He had the charism that helped people get closer to each other." Father Niewęgłowski, who was assigned with him to a parish, adds, "He was not at all like a guide or an orator, but he had the gift of personal contact. He brought intimacy, serenity. He loved small group meetings. He knew how to listen."

Saints are wonderworkers. In every person they are able to reveal hidden talents, to discern the treasure buried beneath the earthen vessel. Their presence stimulates, warms, kindles, and enlightens. Around them, everything goes up a notch: people want to be better! Father Jerzy was like that in his simplicity, in his ordinariness, too, because he really was a common man. A poor speaker, rather frail physically, and hardly prone to great intellectual flights, he nevertheless drew many people to himself. He gave confidence; he touched hearts. Through his way of living shone something of the beauty and tenderness of God. He had a special charism for helping persons who were somewhat lost, depressed, paralyzed with despair; he communicated to them the strength of the Lord. I find this moving because this gift of consolation is something we have in common.

At the age of thirty-two, Father Jerzy was sent to Saint Anne Church. Located next to the major universities in Warsaw, the parish was the center of the pastoral mission for the students in the capital. It was a place of intellectual ferment where young people gathered. The catechesis of the medical students and the chaplaincy of the hospitals in Warsaw were entrusted to him. His ministry therefore put him in ongoing contact with future physicians, the sick, and also with paramedics: stretcher-bearers, ambulance personnel, nurses . . . Because of his own stays in the hospital, he greatly appreciated this milieu, the Gospel values of self-giving and care for the weakest that are expressed in it. He once wrote in an interview: "The medical milieu deserves more pastoral care. The professions of nurse and physician are a true vocation, the ones closest to the priesthood, in fact; they bring mercy to those who need it most: the sick and the suffering. The latter are the most valiant part of the Church: through their sufferings and crosses, they are the closest to Christ."

In 1979, the winds of history, the first gusts of which he had felt during his military service, began to blow again in his life. On the occasion of the first pilgrimage of Pope John Paul II to his native land, Jerzy, because of his familiarity with the medical world, was put in charge of organizing first-aid stations that would be set up all along the route that the Holy Father would travel.

Recall that Karol Wojtyła, the cardinal archbishop of

Warsaw, had been elected pope one year earlier, on October 16, 1978. For the leaders of the Soviet Union, who were well informed about the pontiff's ties with Polish Catholic intellectuals who were hostile to the regime and with Cardinal Wyszyński, the symbol of the popular legitimacy that had been trampled on by Communist ideology, this election was a bombshell. The first words of John Paul II during the inaugural Mass of his pontificate did not prove them wrong: "Do not be afraid. . . . Open the boundaries of States, economic and political systems." On the other hand, the news was welcomed as a breath of fresh air by the Poles, who were suffocating under the lid of oppression on all sides: opposition from intellectuals and laborers was muzzled, freedom of expression was curtailed, society was made politically atheistic, the economy was fettered, travel abroad was reduced to a trickle . . . The pope's arrival strengthened the validity of their struggle for freedom, of which the violently suppressed revolts of 1956, 1968, and 1970 had been the prelude.

Since the earliest days of his pontificate, the pope had planned a visit to the land that had witnessed his birth.[1] He wanted to lend his support to the "Church of silence" that had "its lips closed and its hands tied", as Pius XII put it, and to breach the wall of totalitarianism. By chance the calendar provided him with an occasion: in June 1979, Poland was to commemorate the 900th anniversary of the martyrdom of Saint Stanisław, Bishop of Kraków, who had been assassinated in 1079 by King Bolesław II for refusing to bend to his authority. With a very sure sense of

---

[1] For a behind-the-scenes look at this papal journey, see Bernard Lecomte, *Les Secrets du Vatican* (Paris: Tempus, 2011), 230ff.

politics, the pope thus chose to make his first visit in a situation that recalled one of the most violent conflicts between Church and State in all of Polish history.

When he disembarked at the airport in Okęcie on June 2, 1979, and kissed the ground of his native land, Poland uneasily held its breath: how would this reunion occurring under high surveillance play out? Along the itinerary that led the pontiff to the heart of Warsaw, the gold and white of the Vatican pennants mingled with the red of the Polish flags, as though all of a sudden the nation was rediscovering its colors. The remarks that triggered a peaceful revolution were pronounced on Victory Square, where almost one million Poles were keeping warm. Facing them, alone on the platform, in his little white alb, the pope defied the authorities by proclaiming in his inimitable voice: "No one can exclude Christ from the history of mankind, anywhere on Earth." These words immediately unleashed shouts of enthusiasm. For the duration of a homily, the square became a space of freedom for Poles who rediscovered their confidence. Jerzy was in their midst, in one of the first rows. He was throwing himself wholeheartedly into the mission that had been entrusted to him: supervising the first-aid stations for the pilgrims. He was physically exhausted but happy, profoundly happy about this fellowship between the people and this pope, the pride of a Catholic nation that was reconnecting with its roots.

After Warsaw, the Holy Father traveled to Gniezno, the cradle of Polish Christianity, then to Częstochowa, the beating heart of Catholicism in the country, and finally to Auschwitz, "the Golgotha of the modern world", welcomed each time by a fervent crowd and by volleys of applause. He finished his stay in Kraków with the celebration of a Mass in honor of Saint Stanisłaus. One and a half million Catholics traveled to the event. The pope said to them:

> You must be strong with the strength of *faith*. You must be faithful. Today more than in any other age you need this strength. . . . So, before going away, I beg you once again to accept the whole of the spiritual legacy which goes by the name of "Poland". . . . Never lose your trust, do not be defeated, do not be discouraged. . . . I beg you . . . always *seek* spiritual power from him from whom countless generations of our fathers and mother[s] have found it. *Never detach yourselves* from him, *never lose your spiritual freedom*, with which "he makes a human being free."[2]

For one week, as though they were awaking from a bad dream, millions of Poles realized, from one Mass to the next, that despite thirty years of oppression, the Communist regime had not affected their faith, their identity, or their solidarity. Exhorted by the pope to "be not afraid", they became aware of their numbers and their strength.

Somewhere in that crowd, one man heard as a personal calling the pope's invitation to spiritual resistance. Jerzy Popiełuszko's destiny was in the process of being sealed.

[2] John Paul II, Homily during the papal Mass in honor of Saint Stanisłaus, Kraków, June 10, 1979.

3

The Polish Summer

*The Lord sent me to preach good news
to the poor, to proclaim release to the cap-
tives and recovering of sight to the blind,
to set at liberty those who are oppressed,
to proclaim the acceptable year of the
Lord.*

—Cf. Luke 4:18–19

He had finally thrown in the towel and no longer believed
it possible. After all, the Communist authorities gave these
permissions on very rare occasions, did they not? And
then his status as a priest did not weigh in his favor. Nevertheless, Jerzy was not dreaming: after endless months of
waiting, the visa that he had so much hoped for was right
there in front of his eyes. In a few days he could take a
plane for the first time in his life. Destination: Pittsburgh,
Pennsylvania, where one of his aunts who had settled in
the United States was inviting him to get some rest. This
was in early June 1980. Several days earlier he had received
his new assignment. In order to spare the failing health of
his protégé, Cardinal Wyszyński had appointed him assistant pastor of the parish of Saint Stanisław Kostka in
Żoliborz, a northern district of Warsaw. While continuing his activities as chaplain to the medical milieu, Jerzy's

mission was to assist Father Teofil Bogucki in that parish, which was one of the centers of intellectual life in the capital, where artists, writers, and journalists mingled with laborers from the imposing steelworks nearby, which was called Huta Warszawa. "That will be a different sort of work", Father Popiełuszko had been content to tell himself, not knowing that his life had just taken an abrupt turn and that this little church, where I had the opportunity to celebrate a Mass, was to be the theater where the tragedy of his life would begin.

Meanwhile, there he was in the Boeing 747, departing for the United States. It was June 7, 1980. This was the first time that Jerzy had left his native land. In the airplane, he looked with amazement at everything surrounding him: "The Boeing is colossal. Up front, first class. Salon, bar, piano: every comfort. The lunch is plentiful: bread, butter, cheese, roast beef, potato, a chocolate mint, all washed down with a little beer. I put the pepper and salt into my pocket. I am seated in the middle rows, so that I cannot look through the window, but just the same I see the dazzling brilliance of the sun. We are flying above the clouds." [1]

This trip to America reveals a character that is offhand and carefree, with a zest for life and always on the lookout for little pleasures along the way. "I tried to play bingo, but without success. I have a lot of luck in my life, but not at gambling", he scrawled in his journal. A long road trip down the East Coast then led him to Florida, where, under a blazing sun, he looked for shells on the beach in Tampa. "I covered myself with sunscreen to develop my tan", he writes in his personal notebooks, which are actually the journal of an average tourist. All the stops

---

[1] Jerzy Popiełuszko, *Carnets intimes (1980–1984)* (Paris: Cana, 1988), 2.

are recorded, even the most conventional: nights in mo-
tels, lunch at McDonald's, guided tours of must-see places
like Cape Canaveral, Orlando, not to mention Disney-
land, which the priest found breathtaking: "impossible to
describe", he writes, "you have to experience it, especially
the parade at night: what a fantastic thing!" Sometimes
we imagine that the saints are uncommon, ethereal beings,
freed from material circumstances, immersed in perpetual
prayer; the matter-of-fact journal of Father Jerzy reminds
us that they are cut from the same cloth as we are . . .

When he returned in mid-July 1980, he scarcely recognized his country, which was on the verge of chaos. The
regime had ordered an increase in the price of foodstuffs.
For the Poles, already suffocated by the economic crisis,
it was the last straw. Anger exploded. On July 10, a general strike was declared in Lublin. Within a few weeks,
work stoppages proliferated, paralyzing several parts of
the country. The people were sick and tired of suffering injustice. They demanded changes. On August 14, the
movement took a decisive turn: under the influence of
a young electrician named Lech Wałęsa, the workers in
the "Lenin" shipyard of Gdańsk stopped working in turn.
During the night, representatives from around twenty factories in the country formed a common strike committee
—which was to become the union Solidarność—and put
Wałęsa at the head of it. On August 15, the strike extended to other working-class cities on the Baltic shore.
In order to avoid contagion, the Communist authorities
cut the telephone lines between the coast and the rest of
Poland. Too late: the conflict spread like wildfire. Right
away the movement was marked with the seal of solidarity. The strikers in Gdańsk thus refused to sign an agreement with the government so as not to leave out their

comrades on smaller construction sites who had no chance of pleading their cause alone. Interdependent, massive, joyous, even festive, these strikes also proudly proclaimed their connection with the Christian faith, which was a novelty in comparison with earlier uprisings of workers: East Berlin in 1953, Budapest and Poznań in 1956, Gdynia in 1970, Radom in 1976 . . . On the archive photographs, the blue-collar workers from Gdańsk appear kneeling before makeshift altars, during open-air Masses, under the smoking chimneys of the factories. The viewer can see hanging on the gates at the entrances images of Our Lady of Częstochowa and of Pope John Paul II, whose exhortation, "Be not afraid" was on everyone's mind. Precisely on August 22, the pope lent his support to the workers in a letter to Cardinal Wyszyński. In it he mentioned the "difficult struggle of the Polish nation to assure its daily bread, social justice, and its inalienable right to a life of its own".[2] In Gniezno, the primate of the Polish hierarchy, while likewise taking a firm stance in support of the strikers, nevertheless recommended prudence: the threat of Soviet intervention loomed at every moment. Since the crushing of the Prague Spring in 1968, the Socialist countries had been living with the status of "limited sovereignty" invented by Brezhnev: specifically, any political excess within one of the "brother countries" was considered a threat to the other countries and could result in military repression. On August 26, in the presence of thousands of pilgrims gathered in Częstochowa, the primate emphasized the justice of the workers' demands, but made an appeal for calm in order to avoid the invasion of the country by Russian troops. But on the 28th, the strikes

---

[2] Letter quoted by Bernard Lecomte in "'So-li-darnosc!': Comment le pape polonais a renversé le cours de l'histoire", in *Les Secrets du Vatican* (Paris: Tempus, 2011), 239.

spread to Wrocław and Kraków, and by the 29th they had reached the whole country.

In Warsaw, in the immense Huta Warszawa steelworks, the workers stopped production at the end of August. Shut away on the premises of the factory that they were occupying day and night, they demanded Masses. "August 31 fell on a Sunday, in other words a feast day," recalls Karol Szadurski, one of the workers at the site, "and a great number of us submitted to the strike committee our request to have a Mass said right there on the premises of the occupied steelworks."

A delegation of workers called on Cardinal Wyszyński to demand a priest. The primate's secretary asked several, but they all declined. In Saint Stanisłaus parish, a young, just-appointed assistant pastor volunteered: Father Popiełuszko . . . On August 31, Jerzy advanced timidly toward the gate of the factory, his heart tormented by worries. Later he wrote:

> I will never forget that day or the Mass that I said. I was terribly nervous; I had never been in a situation like that. What sort of atmosphere would I find? How would they receive me? Where would I celebrate the Mass? Who would read the readings, who would sing? Questions like that, which today appear naïve to me, tormented me then, as I was heading toward the factory. At the doors of the steelworks, I had my first major shock. A dense crowd was waiting for me, smiling and in tears at the same time. They applauded me, and I thought for a moment that a celebrity was walking behind me. But no, the applause was actually meant for me, the first priest who had ever walked through the entrance of the steelworks. I told myself then that they were giving an ovation to the Church that for thirty years had been knocking on the doors of the factories. All my apprehension proved to be groundless: the altar had been prepared in

the middle of the square as well as a cross that then was erected at the entrance and, after surviving the darkest days, still stands there, surrounded by flowers. Even a makeshift confessional had been set up. The lectors were there, too. You had to listen to them, those hoarse voices accustomed to swear words, solemnly reading the sacred texts. Then from thousands of mouths came a cry like thunder: "Thanks be to God." I noticed also that they knew how to sing, and better than in the churches. Before beginning, they went to confession. I was sitting on a chair, with my back leaning against a heap of scrap iron, and these rough men in blue work clothes spotted with grease knelt down on the dirty, oil-stained floor.[3]

For Jerzy it was a revelation, the turning point of his life! On the photographs that immortalized the scene, he appears radiant, peaceful, almost liberated, holding in one hand a safety helmet and in the other flowers offered by the strikers. Surrounded by workers, he beamed with joy, as though he had finally found his apostolate, the vineyard where the Lord wanted him to work. Yes, he would be the priest for those men, those pious workers who needed a pastor to give them courage, to show them the way, and to lead them to God.

After weeks of extreme tension, the Polish summer ended in an apotheosis. On August 31, in front of cameras from all over the world, Lech Wałęsa signed the Gdańsk agreements with a pen depicting John Paul II in order to advertise his Christian faith. Throughout the world there was astonishment: for the first time in the history of the Communist bloc, a government tolerated the existence of free labor unions, independent of the Party, and ac-

---

[3] Quoted by Jean Offredo, "À Dieu Jerzy!", in Jerzy Popiełuszko, *Le Chemin de ma croix: Messes à Varsovie* (Paris: Cana, 1984), 6.

knowledged the right to strike. And the arm-wrestling
that pitted the government against the strikers had caused
no casualties. On the shore of the Baltic Sea, in the major
industrial cities, they did not even record an exchange
of punches. For the union Solidarność, which was officially born at that moment, it was a historic victory.
"Thank you, thank you!" the crowd shouted, uplifted by
the hope that Poland was finally regaining a human face
and the prospect of better days. The word *Solidarność*,
which means "solidarity", was on everyone's lips, and
new memberships poured in. Out of the thirteen million
workers in the country, ten were affiliated with the union
in just a few weeks. This dynamic galvanized the Poles.
"We felt united", recalls Wojciech Olejnik, a metallurgist
from Huta Warszawa. "Ten million people were a force
with which the regime was going to have to contend.
Never before in our history had it been possible to as-
semble such a federation."

In order to understand the workings of this great popular movement, we must not be misled by the terms. As
the demands indicate—respect for civil rights, pluralism,
liberation of political prisoners—Solidarność was not a
labor union in the sense that we in the West understand
it, most often as a movement to defend professional interests. Although it was indeed rooted in a struggle for
the dignity of workers, the movement spread its branches
far beyond that. It brought together individuals from all
over the political scene, from very different generations
and social milieus. It was a happy mixture of workers
and intellectuals, Christians and atheists, students and re-
tirees, cities and rural areas, as though the whole Polish
nation, whose union had become its legitimate represen-
tative, was confronting Marxist totalitarianism directly.
"Solidarność embodied popular legitimacy over against

the legality of the Communist authorities", comments the journalist Jean Offredo,[4] who was the French editor of Jerry Popiełuszko and Lech Wałęsa. Father Jerzy said the same two years later when he remembered those days in August 1980 "when the solidarity of the Polish nation was born". He continues:

> We were kneeling, rosary in hand, in front of makeshift altars, with patriotic and religious songs on our lips. Born of the patriotic surge of the workers, supported by the intellectuals and the cultural circles, Solidarność is a union of hearts, minds, and hands, rooted in ideals capable of transforming the world. It is the hope of millions of Poles, a hope that is that much stronger because it flows from the source of all hope, I mean: God.[5]

As expected, the Communist authorities did not delay in reacting. For Moscow, the Gdańsk agreements were a bombshell. It was impossible to ratify the existence of this independent labor union, which attacked the dogma of the "leading role" of the Party in the functioning of society and introduced dangerous cracks in the walls of the system. The Holy Father, who was following the events from the Vatican, was worried about a Soviet counter-offensive. As early as September 3, he mentioned "the moral right of Poland to sovereignty and independence" and prayed that his country might not be "the victim of any aggression from whatever source".[6] In December 1980, the Warsaw Pact countries, vassals to Moscow, organized military maneuvers at the gates of the country. It was a way of intimidating the Poles by evoking the

---

[4] "La foi prise au mot" [Faith taken at its word], a radio program devoted to Jerzy Popiełuszko broadcast by KTO, March 2012.

[5] Homily at the Mass for the fatherland, August 1982, in Popiełuszko, *Chemin de ma croix*, 41–42.

[6] John Paul II, General Audience, Castel Gandolfo, September 3, 1980.

memory of the invasion of Czechoslovakia by the Red Army in 1968. While they were at it, the Polish government decided to break the Gdańsk agreements. The militants of Solidarność were worried and often arrested. In response, the strikes resumed with a vengeance. An arm-wrestling match began, and no one knew the outcome.

In that heavy atmosphere of threats, Father Popiełuszko was appointed chaplain of the steelworks in the Polish capital, while keeping his assignment as assistant pastor at Saint Stanisłaus. For him it was the beginning of a daily, constant involvement alongside the strikers of Huta Warszawa and their families, during the five hundred days that the Solidarność adventure lasted. Sacrificing his personal time, his rest, and his health, he went to the factory every morning to hear the strikers' confessions, strengthen their hope, channel their violence, purify their hatred, and encourage them never to give in to fear. "The only fear that we should have", he said, "is of being cut off from God." For these thousands of workers, whose claims he espoused, Father Jerzy served as a guide and a moral compass. He appeared also as the symbol of the union between the Church and the workers' movement, a union sealed by the blessing of the banner of Solidarność in a moving ceremony that assembled more than twenty thousand strikers in front of Saint Stanisłaus Kostka Church in April 1981. Rarely had ecclesial communion been felt with such intensity: the Church was in the midst of her people, who commended themselves entirely to God. Over the course of his apostolate, Jerzy established ties of friendship with Lech Wałęsa, the national hero of the movement, whom he met several times. Without joining the executive board of Solidarność, he became, along with other priests like Father Jankowski, a chaplain of the movement in Gdańsk, one of its great spiritual leaders. There was another side of the coin: this display drew the attention of the authorities, who were on their guard.

The entire year 1981 was a crescendo of tension. Not until the month of November did the conflict become a little less heated. Finally, a resolution appeared to be feasible. Everybody was holding his breath: General Jaruzelski, who headed the government, agreed to sit down at the table with Cardinal Glemp, the new primate of Poland,[7] and Lech Wałęsa, the head of Solidarność, to discuss an agreement. But under pressure from the Kremlin, which wanted nothing to do with negotiations, the compromise fell apart. From then on the situation was hanging by a thread. At any moment it could degenerate, turn sour, and veer into violence. In fact, after several weeks of indecision, tanks entered the major cities of the country in the night between December 12 and 13. While he was at it, General Jaruzelski spoke out on television. On screens throughout the country, his gloomy face appeared, with his round glasses, receding hairline, and khaki uniform covered with decorations. The military officer solemnly declared: "I address you as a soldier and as the head of the Polish government. The situation is serious. Our fatherland is on the brink of the abyss."[8] The general continued, saying essentially that the only way out of the chaos was to take exceptional measures. And so he declared a state of siege, with the accompanying host of coercive mea-

---

[7] Cardinal Stefan Wyszyński, Jerzy's "spiritual father", died on May 28, 1981.

[8] General Jaruzelski, televised speech, December 13, 1981.

sures: a ban on strikes, public demonstrations, and free-doms, the militarization of public life, the arrest of polit-ical opponents, and sealing the borders completely. With an iron hand, the general took control of the country. Thousands of persons were imprisoned, including Lech Wałęsa. In the streets, the ZOMO, anti-riot units that specialized in tracking down political opponents, made their appearance. The roads bristled with barbed-wire fences, searches became routine, and raids were intensi-fied. Almost five hundred days after its birth, Solidarność was made illegal.

As the year 1982 began, General Jaruzelski's armed take-over seemed to be a success. Order had been restored, calm prevailed in the streets. But discreetly, clandestinely, a spiritual resistance was being prepared. Jerzy was at the outposts of it. "Truth is unchangeable," he said to the workers, "it cannot be destroyed by decrees." [9]

---

[9] Homily given at the Mass for the fatherland, October 1982, in Popiełuszko, *Chemin de ma croix*, 57.

4

The "Masses for the Fatherland"

> *I send you out as sheep in the midst of wolves.*
>
> —Matthew 10:16

A regime that needs weapons to stay in existence dies by itself. Its violence is the proof of its moral inferiority. If Solidarność won hearts, it was not by struggling with power but by offering resistance on its knees, with a rosary in hand. In front of outdoor altars, it demanded the dignity of human work, freedom of conscience, and respect for man. Solidarność is a mighty tree: its top has been removed, and its branches have been cut, but its roots are deeply rooted among us, and new branches will grow back.[1]

The man who stood up this way to the dictatorship and threw in its face these sentences that flap like a flag in a stiff breeze was not a politician or a military leader, but a young priest of the Catholic Church whose only ammunition was his courage and the Holy Spirit. A prelate who was acquainted with Father Popiełuszko during that crucial period of martial law remembers a

---

[1] Homily, Mass for the fatherland, December 1982, in Jerzy Popiełuszko, *Le Chemin de ma croix: Messes à Varsovie* (Paris: Cana, 1984), 74.

metamorphosis: "Thanks to the tragic events of December 1981, a timid, somewhat awkward young man became a confident, courageous leader, as though a new spirit had entered into him." It is often said that in order to develop, "great men" need the compost of exceptional circumstances. It took General Jaruzelski's coup d'état and the violent acts committed against the workers who were so dear to his apostolic heart to make the young assistant pastor reveal himself, draw himself up to his full height, and decide to throw himself body and soul into the resistance movement . . .

The word "resistance" automatically evokes images of armed struggle and underground activity. Jerzy belies that notion. "My weapon is truth and love", he used to say in speaking about his opposition to the regime, against which he never lifted the smallest firearm. The theater of his dissent was the modest parish of Saint Stanisłaus Kostka. Nor was his resistance fomented in a smoke-filled back room: it operated in the daylight, behind the altar of the church where, from February 1982 on, he celebrated his famous "Masses for the fatherland".

These Masses went back to the early nineteenth century when the country had disappeared from the map of Europe, divided among tsarist Russia, Prussia, and the Austro-Hungarian Empire. For almost 120 years, between 1795 and 1918, Poland became a nation without a State. In order to destroy the country at its roots, the occupants then forbade the Poles to use their own language. The Church soon became the spearhead of resistance to this policy of eradication. It organized clandestine Masses in order to keep the fatherland alive. Celebrated in Polish in crypts that were shielded from surveillance, these litur-

gies were sprinkled with references to the nation's literary patrimony and to the great hours of its history. As
guardians of "Polishness", the priests were persuaded that
Poland would get through the crisis by remaining faithful to its culture and its spiritual, immaterial patrimony.
This tradition was kept up during the German occupation, between 1939 and 1945, only to come back again
under Communism, especially after the state of siege. So
it happened that in February 1982, in Warsaw, Father
Bogucki, the pastor of Saint Stanisław, assigned Jerzy to
organize these "Masses for the fatherland", which under
the influence of the young assistant pastor would have
unprecedented repercussions.

This brings us to late February 1982. It was seven o'clock
in the evening. The Church of Saint Stanisław was bursting at the seams. It was Father Jerzy's first "Mass for the
fatherland". Alone in the sacristy, where he could hear
the murmuring of the faithful, the assistant pastor felt
a mixture of apprehension and confidence. Confidence
because he knew that he had the support of the hierarchy, which had just published a statement supporting
Solidarność: "The Church always sides with the truth
and with people in trouble. Today, therefore, she is with
those who have been deprived of freedom and whose conscience has been violated."[2] No doubt the pope's words,
uttered during a recent Angelus message, were also echoing in his head. In it the Holy Father recalled the right of
workers to enjoy their civil liberties: "This is an important question, not only for a particular country, but for

[2] Statement by the Polish bishops and the primate of Poland, cited by Jerzy
during the Mass for the fatherland in February 1982, in Popiełuszko, *Chemin
de ma croix*, 3.

human history", John Paul II insisted. "For this reason Solidarność is part of the patrimony of all nations."[3] At peace with his conscience, Jerzy knew that he was serving a just cause. But he doubted himself. Would he be up to the people's hopes? Would he find words to lighten their troubles? And then where would he find the courage to confront the police, since he knew that members of it were concealed in the crowd? The clock sounded the end of this shilly-shallying. A silence as though in a cathedral came over the congregation. After the sign of the cross, Jerzy started the liturgy. His voice was calm and confident:

> We gather in the name of Jesus Christ to place our prayers on Christ's altar, but also everything that it has been granted us to endure in this trial of the whole nation. We include in particular those who have been most painfully affected by the state of martial law, those who have been deprived of freedom, arrested, interned, laid off—both them and their families. We include even those who are in the service of lies and injustice.[4]

Father Popiełuszko was in charge of preparing these Masses. He understood the confidence that the Poles could draw from them. He paid particular attention to the biblical readings and all the other texts that are worked into the liturgy. The entrance antiphons were often taken from the Romantic poetry of the nineteenth century, when the Polish poets dipped their pens into the Christian faith to beg for the liberation of their occupied fatherland. After Communion, one heard the "classics" of the national lit-

---

[3] John Paul II, Angelus message, December 20, 1981.

[4] Introduction to the liturgy of the Mass for the fatherland, February 1982, in Popiełuszko, *Chemin de ma croix*, 2.

erature, selected for their patriotic and religious inspiration. These great texts were often read by famous actors. Father Jerzy wanted these celebrations to be a crucible in which all the social strata of the nation would be mixed, the workers of course, but also the actors, the intellectuals, the directors, and the men of letters. Sometimes contemporary documents were offered for the prayer of the faithful, like this letter by a mother to her son who was sentenced to eight years in prison because of the state of martial law: "You can imprison the body but never the spirit! No, nobody can lock up lofty human thought, or the heart that suffers for its native land, or the faith of our ancestors, or the expectation of the children, or the feelings that weld together the unity of a people. May neither simple solidarity nor faith ever be lacking! And the Lord will say: Let there be Poland!"[5]

Finally, Jerzy not infrequently gave a place of honor to texts that evoked the thousand-year history of Poland, which sometimes gave his Masses the appearance of true history courses. Thus to the left of the altar, beside the flag of Solidarność, he set up a large chronological frieze depicting the chief popular uprisings. This was a way of including the contemporary era in those long centuries and of calling Christians to be confident: "You see, in other moments, our country was exposed to misfortune, but by drawing on its faith, it always got through it!"[6]

But obviously the religious dimension was at the center of these liturgies. Basing his homilies on the writings

[5] Homily at the Mass for the fatherland, December 1982, in Popiełuszko, *Chemin de ma croix*, 77.

[6] This insistence on the history of the Polish nation is particularly evident in the homily at the Mass for the fatherland in November 1983, in Popiełuszko, *Chemin de ma croix*, 153ff.

of John Paul II and Cardinal Wyszyński and on the social doctrine of the Church, Father Jerzy revealed the aspirations to truth, freedom, fraternity, justice, and union with God that dwell in the heart of every man. He recalled the eminent dignity of the human person, which was jeopardized by the Communist regime. "Freedom is a value that God has inscribed in man since his creation. Failure to respect this right is an act against the Creator himself. As children of God, we cannot be slaves. Our divine affiliation bears within it the heritage of freedom, especially freedom of conscience and of opinion." [7]

Although he lashed out at the violation of consciences by the police authorities, his teaching also revealed the true nature of justice, which finds its source in God. He concluded: "It is impossible to speak about justice . . . where the word 'God' has been officially eliminated from the life of the fatherland. Let us be aware of the unlawfulness and prejudice that are inflicted on our Christian nation when it is made atheistic by law, when they destroy in the souls of the children the Christian values that their parents have instilled in them from the cradle." [8]

This critique of Marxist anti-Christian sentiment is one of the recurring themes of his homilies. "The prevalent policy is an absurd, stubborn attempt to take God away from people and to impose on them an ideology that has nothing in common with our Christian tradition. This programmed atheism, this struggle against God and all that is holy, is at the same time a struggle against human

[7] Homily at the Mass for the fatherland, August 1983, in Popiełuszko, *Chemin de ma croix*, 50.

[8] Jerzy Popiełuszko, *Méditations du chapelet* (Bydgoszcz, October 19, 1984). The text is reprinted as an appendix to this book.

greatness and dignity; for man is great because he bears within himself the dignity of the children of God."[9]

For Jerzy, although the current regime was seeking to stifle its profound identity, Poland had the right to exist in its cultural specificity. The way that the country would survive the loss of its independence was through its culture. He repeatedly told the faithful:

> Polish culture is a good that defines us more than material forces or political boundaries. Spiritually, our nation has always been independent, even when it was occupied, because it possessed its magnificent culture. Today, it is necessary to demand courageously the right to our national culture and heritage. We cannot forget our Christian past. We cannot cut off the roots of our more than thousand-year history, because a tree without roots collapses.[10]

But first of all it was truth, the splendor of truth, that motivated the quest of Father Popiełuszko, who put all his efforts into flushing out the lies of the dictatorship.

> Truth contains within itself the ability to resist and to blossom in the light of day, even if they try very diligently and carefully to hide it. The men who proclaim the truth do not need to be numerous. Christ, incidentally, surrounded himself with a small number of individuals. Falsehood is what requires a lot of people, because it always needs to be renewed and fed. Our duty as Christians is to abide in the truth, even if it costs dearly.[11]

[9] Homily at the Mass for the fatherland, September 1982, in Popiełuszko, *Chemin de ma croix*, 50.

[10] Homily at the Mass for the fatherland, September 1983, in Popiełuszko, *Chemin de ma croix*, 141.

[11] Homily at the Mass for the fatherland, September 1982, in Popiełuszko, *Chemin de ma croix*, 50.

The content of these Masses left no one indifferent, even within the Polish clergy. Father Piotr Nitecki, who would concelebrate several of them with Jerzy, remembers his initial mistrust.

> At the start, my feelings were mixed. I had heard that they resembled demonstrations in opposition to the authorities. Now, the Eucharist is a sacrament, and the pulpit should not be mistaken for the podium at a meeting. And then I went, and I understood that this was a question of evangelization, not of politics. This Mass was celebrated on a balcony in front of the church in the presence of an immense crowd of believers. Father Jerzy's teaching was a great event. I heard in his homilies the universal message of the Church, proclaimed within the context of the blatant violation of human dignity by the totalitarian system that was characteristic of that era. It was not politics but the proclamation of Jesus Christ, the Truth who makes us free.

Soon Father Jerzy's Masses became the focal point of all hopes. Clandestine militants of Solidarność, relatives and friends of the imprisoned, and residents of Warsaw came to recover their zeal and to experience freedom. "Truth resounded in the church", Karol Szadurski, a former employee of the Huta Warszawa steelworks recalls. "I do not know whether it occupied more than a hectare [2.5 acres], but we got the impression of having at our disposal there a bit of free Poland." Katarzyna Soborak, a friend of Jerzy, continues: "We prayed with all our hearts that the situation in the country would improve. And when the people started to sing, "Lord, hear our prayer", they would look at each other and burst into tears, sobbing. Among us true solidarity reigned; it was extraordinary."

Drawn by word of mouth, the crowd became more im-
pressive each month. Sometimes the church was too small
to accommodate it. Then an altar was set up on a terrace
overlooking an immense park where the assembled inhabitants of Warsaw kept warm. Some Masses drew more
than twenty thousand persons, as at a rock concert. In
every corner of the street, police vehicles were posted
to keep an eye on the crowd that was fascinated by the
young assistant pastor whose words, rooted in the Polish
culture and carried by a powerful spiritual breeze, resounded like an affront to the ears of the regime. The laborer Kzadurski recalls: "The importance of these Masses
is reflected in what an officer from the security services
told me one day: 'For us Communists, each of these
Masses is like a lost battle, and if I could, I would kill
you with one blow, you and your Father Popiełuszko,
and that would be the end of it.'"

In late 1982, Jerzy raised the bar even farther. The assistant pastor compared the nation's Calvary to the Passion of Christ, and the arbitrary condemnations of the
Poles to the trial of Jesus, "this trial that is still ongoing
through our brothers, a trial in which all those who try
to build on falsehoods and half-truths participate".[12] Every last Sunday of the month he laid down at the foot of
the Cross the burden of the fatherland and implored the
risen Christ to "change our sorrows and joys into graces of
hope for the victory of good over evil".[13] Seasoned with
chiseled phrases that fed the people's hope and sharpened
their insights, his sermons were like a searchlight tracking

[12] Ibid., 49.
[13] Prayer of the faithful at the Mass for the fatherland, December 1982, in
Jerzy Popiełuszko, *Chemin de ma croix*, 70.

down injustices, the pangs of a bad conscience and the betrayals of memory. He lamented:

> How difficult it is for us to have a pure heart when the system of materialistic propaganda strives to convince us that there is no more life beyond the grave. We must be strong to resist those who want to build our fatherland on materialistic, ephemeral foundations, those who instill atheism in minds. Our nation, rooted in its Christian tradition, will always aspire to full freedom. And a Pole who loves God and the fatherland will get up from any humiliation because he kneels before God alone.[14]

The assistant pastor also took special care with the prayer of the faithful, which he himself composed. Here for example are the petitions recited during the Mass in October 1982:

> Let us pray for our martyred fatherland; for those who are deprived of freedom, arrested, condemned, imprisoned, that they may regain their freedom and resume the tasks that society has entrusted to them; for those who have lost their lives or health during the state of martial law, may their suffering hasten the coming of a free and just Poland; for those who are in the service of falsehood and injustice, that God may open their hearts and help them to see the truth of their humiliation; for the soldiers of the Polish army, that they may never stain their uniform and their honor by raising a hand against their nation; for us gathered here in prayer, that we may never lose hope in the victory of good that is being prepared in suffering, we pray to the Lord.[15]

[14] Jerzy Popiełuszko, "Meditation on the Way of the Cross" during a workers' pilgrimage to the Shrine of Częstochowa on September 28, 1983, in Jerzy Popiełuszko, *Carnets intimes (1980–1984)* (Paris: Cana, 1988), 64–65.

[15] Prayer of the faithful at the Mass for the fatherland, October 1982, in Popiełuszko, *Chemin de ma croix*, 60–61.

These simple, profound prayers came to grips with the everyday difficulties of the Poles and therefore touched their hearts, consoled them in their sorrows, and stirred up their hope.

Jerzy's fame grew day by day. Soon the echo of his sermons extended beyond the city limits of Warsaw to the farthest reaches of the country. His homilies were recorded on cassette tapes or transcribed and mimeographed, then published in newspapers that circulated clandestinely. His courage and devotion became legendary. We know that he attended all the sham trials brought against the opponents of the regime. And that each time the verdict was read out, he stood up, turned his back to the judge and intoned the national anthem. We know also that at Saint Stanisław parish he organized distributions of medications and food, helped the imprisoned activists, and offered aid to their families. "His cassock was always incompletely buttoned, as though he had not finished getting dressed. He was always in a hurry, always running somewhere", Joanna Szczepkowska, an actress friend, recalls.

During those confusing days when all the landmarks were being blown up, Father Popiełuszko pointed to safe paths and marked out itineraries so that the faithful would not go astray. "He helped us to discern the signs of the times, to understand the age in which we were living. His preaching enabled us to distinguish good and evil", recalls Everyn Kaworski, a former member of Solidarność. For the faithful who were lost in the middle of all these upheavals, the present appeared foggy and the future, uncertain. But Jerzy made sense of this chaos. Thanks to his homilies, the canvas of their lives stopped looking like the wrong side of a tapestry, with its multitude of knots and zigzagging threads: although they could see neither the value nor the meaning of it, he provided them with a motive.

Father Jerzy's Masses for the fatherland resounded also with his tireless exhortations to keep the peace. "Go your separate ways in recollection; do not listen to the provocateurs who are trying to get you to demonstrate or to chant. Only one thing brought us here: the good of our fatherland and our common prayer for it",[16] the priest would exclaim, afraid that the end of these Masses might veer into a fistfight. No call for revenge ever came from his lips, but only invitations to forgiveness and reconciliation. "Sometimes", a Catholic who attended these Masses testifies, "we were aggressively, combatively standing up against the government. Then Father exhorted us to love our adversaries, and the people gave up their hatred. I personally was truly disarmed by that priest." During that period of tension, Father Popiełuszko based his position firmly on the course of action described in a letter of Saint Paul: "Do not be overcome by evil, but overcome evil with good" (Rom 12:21). Responding to the extortions and provocations with hatred was out of the question; he called instead for an increase of love. The assistant pastor reminded his friends of this unceasingly: at the end of our life, we will be judged by our love!

In his *Divine Comedy*, Dante has this phrase inscribed over the entrance to hell: "Abandon all hope, you who enter here." Conscious that the lack of hope is the worst thing of all, Jerzy embellished each of his homilies with strong doses of optimism, especially when times became

---

[16] Mass for the fatherland, February 1983, in Popiełuszko, *Chemin de ma croix*, 90.

stormy and the horizon was obstructed. "Good is like the seed sown in the earth: first it takes root, then one day it pierces through the soil", he used to say to inspire people with confidence.[17] Of course, Solidarność had sustained a severe blow, and the open wound was still bleeding. "Yet," he continued, "this is not a mortal wound, because it is impossible to kill hope. Now Solidarność is still the hope of millions of Poles, a hope that is that much stronger because it is close to God through prayer."[18]

For the regime, Father Popiełuszko was like a thorn in the flesh. His homilies were intolerable provocations. Surveillance tightened around the young priest who was becoming more annoying every day. During his Masses, informants came to mingle with the faithful. You could spot them immediately: they did not know how to make the sign of the cross and knelt down at the wrong times. "The political authorities cannot get over these liturgies; they say that they are the largest meetings under martial law", Jerzy remarked, not without a bit of malice.[19] Henryk Wujec, a leader in Solidarność, confirms it: "The regime detested these Masses because the people came to them to gain strength, like a man who comes to drink water at a well and leaves reassured and courageous." At the end of his patience, the minister of the interior decided to resort to dirty tricks. Jerzy's sermons were falsified by the security services, which also published false accusa-

[17] Jerzy Popiełuszko, "Meditation on the Way of the Cross" during a workers' pilgrimage to the Shrine of Częstochowa on September 28, 1983, in Popiełuszko, *Carnets intimes*, 64.

[18] Homily at a Mass for the fatherland, August 1982, in Popiełuszko, *Chemin de ma croix*, 42.

[19] November 13, 1982, in Popiełuszko, *Carnets intimes*, 15.

tions to sully his reputation. The priest noted in his journal: "I am in possession of a document from the minister addressed to the archbishop's chancery. They accuse me of activity hostile to Poland. They even accuse the hymns sung during my Masses of being aimed against the State."[20]

The State propaganda machine launched press campaigns to portray him as an activist propagating hatred. It implied that his Masses were disguised political meetings, "anti-government offensives that threaten the system, the capital, and the State". Father Bogucki, the pastor of the parish, stood on the ramparts: "An anarchist, my assistant pastor?! On the contrary, he never stops calling for peace, reason, patience. The proof is that extraordinary calm and seriousness prevail during his worship services."

Under severe pressure at every moment, Jerzy felt that he was being hunted down. He hesitated to answer the telephone in his room, which he knew was bugged. Karol Szadurski, a former laborer at Huta Warszawa, recalls: "He told us all about the dangerous situations that he faced. One day a municipal vehicle drove up in front of him at high speed to try to run him over." On November 18, 1982, he learned that General Jaruzelski talked about imprisoning him if he did not change his attitude. His reaction was both vehement and immediate: "They can imprison me, arrest me, and cause a scandal, but I cannot stop my activity, which is a service rendered to the Church, the fatherland, and my people."[21] During the night between December 13 and 14, at two o'clock in the

[20] Ibid., 21.
[21] Ibid., 16.

morning, an explosive charge broke the windows of his apartment. Jerzy emerged unharmed, but he knew that nothing would be the same now as it had been before. He confided to a friend: "If they want to kill me, they will kill me. On the way to church, or at the rectory, someone will jump out from behind a bush and stab me in the back. They will say that it was a madman. Believe me, if they want to kill me, nothing and no one will prevent them from doing so."

This valiant, determined attitude was like a living catechesis for the Poles. Father Jerzy's courage, the perfect agreement between what he preached and what he was, pricked the consciences of the faithful, who were also impressed by the ardent, living, joyous faith of this young assistant priest whose face emitted a peaceful light. Waldemar Chrostowski, his driver, describes the attraction that he exercised on people: "People sought out his presence, were drawn to him as though to a magnet." It is well known that a person who lives by Jesus attracts others to him. Jerzy's intimate relationship with the Lord was such that his faith spread around him by contagion.

Accounts of conversions brought about in his wake are a recurring feature in his personal journals. Thousands of workers, strikers, men and women of all ages, from all social milieus rediscovered the way of the Church thanks to that young priest. Considering this shower of graces, Jerzy offered to the Lord his humble thanks: "What great things you accomplish, O God, through the intervention of such an unworthy creature as I am. Thank you for making use of me this way!"[22]

---

[22] Ibid., 22.

5

Laying Down His Arms

*When the righteous cry for help, the
Lord hears, and delivers them out of
all their troubles.*

—Psalm 34:17

It is February 3, 1983, at six o'clock in the morning. With
his mind still foggy, Jerzy is at the steering wheel of his
automobile, which is traveling through the deserted streets
of a capital city still numb with sleep. His friends Mar-
garet and Christian are at his side. The little band is headed
south, toward the Tatra range, for a ten-day excursion in
the mountains, where other friends are supposed to meet
them. Exhausted by the tension of recent months, Jerzy
has been looking forward to this break in the great out-
doors for many long weeks. Against a background of mu-
sic spouted by the car radio, the friends exchange the latest
news. While the conversation revolves around road conditions and the weather, Jerzy notices in the rearview mirror
a green Fiat 125 approaching them at high speed. When it
catches up to them, its passengers gesture for him to pull
over. "Two police officers got out of the car", the priest
recalls. "They were very aggressive: 'Your papers. Open
the trunk and your baggage; this is a search.'"[1] The verifi-
cation of the papers was interminable. After several hours

[1] Jerzy Popiełuszko, *Carnets intimes (1980–1984)* (Paris: Cana, 1988), 24–25.

of waiting, Jerzy set out again, followed by a ballet of un-marked cars for dozens of miles.

Over the course of the year 1983, Father Popiełuszko would experience countless provocations of this sort, which rubbed his nerves raw. The police decided to engage in non-stop combat in order to make him bend and to re-duce him to silence. Their imagination was boundless. One night, between one and four in the morning, Jerzy was awakened by a parade of vehicles that circled around his apartment as though in a merry-go-round. The sound of the horns, the humming of the motors, the screech-ing of the tires as a result of sudden braking sowed fear in his mind. "Last night was difficult", he admitted. "They tried to intimidate me by driving like madmen around the rectory." [2] A psychological toll was taken also by the discreet but incessant presence of policemen in civilian garb during services. There was no longer any respite for Jerzy. He lived constantly under the inquisitive gaze of that eye from Moscow. He could not say a word or take a step without being heard, followed, and spied on by those shadowy men. The atmosphere was oppressive, suffocat-ing. But Father Popiełuszko was not one for tragedy, and he knew how to cope with these threats. One day, dur-ing a Mass, he decided to single out the moles and to put the pressure back on them: "I address those who come to these Masses in obedience to orders issued to them. Have a little honesty with your superiors: inform them accu-rately about what you hear and see here, so that your su-periors do not make themselves ridiculous by accusing us of false, fabricated things." [3]

---

[2] Ibid., 21.

[3] Homily at a Mass for the fatherland, March 1983, in Jerzy Popiełuszko, *Le Chemin de ma croix: Messes à Varsovie* (Paris: Cana, 1984), 99.

Another time, on the feast day of the patron saint of miners, he noticed policemen patrolling in the courtyard of the rectory. Some agents were pacing back and forth in front of his door, too, and in the staircase. Indeed, the police wanted to prevent him from going to the church to say Mass for the workers on that potentially explosive day. As often happened, the priest owed his safety to his parishioners, who came to look for him in his apartment to shield him from the government surveillance. Since a grenade had exploded in his room, and given the redoubled threats, the faithful of Saint Stanisłaus organized a sort of Praetorian Guard around him. The most sturdily built men remained on sentry duty in front of his door and stood guard ceaselessly. "The workers from the parish put grills over my window to make it impossible to throw stones into the apartment. Moreover, since December 14, 1982, there is always someone who sleeps in my quarters at night", the assistant pastor noted, moved by these attentions that were the sign of the depth of the bond that had formed between the pastor and his sheep.

Jerzy's personal journals are swarming with intimidations of this sort, which happened by the dozens. The priest was put under maximum pressure. They wanted to break him. Anything was useful to get on his nerves, to unhinge him: telephone surveillance, repeated interrogations, harassment of acquaintances, searches of his apartment, and ceaseless provocations by the police, who stopped him whenever he traveled. Jerzy had no freedom of movement; the surveillance was relentless. After spending months in that atmosphere of instability, shackled by an iron collar of constraints, he was all on edge. He wrote in his journal: "I am at the limits of my physical and psychological resistance. I feel increasingly oppressed by them. But God is good: he gives me mental and physical strength, so much so that it astonishes me, even though I do spend tormented nights."[4]

In the spring of 1983, the morale of the Poles was at half-mast. One and a half years had passed since the country had become bogged down in violence. The state of martial law was prolonged, hopes sank, and courage dwindled. In order to revive the flame, the priest exclaimed:

> Jesus Christ is our companion in misfortune. He shows us how never to lose confidence. And as often happens, our hope, the hope of our unions, of our fatherland, is weakened today. We need you, Lord, to strengthen our hope that victory always belongs to what is good, to what is great, to what is noble, to whatever lives in union with you.[5]

As the recollection of past victories faded, the priest also exhorted the faithful to refresh their memory: "Let us pray to Christ that we may remain faithful to the ideals that we carry in our hearts, the ideals for which we have fought and paid the price of suffering in the heated hours of August 1980."[6]

He himself, however, was not in the best shape. He was going through one of the most difficult periods in his life. Above and beyond the police pressure that was tearing him apart, he had just learned about the assassination by the political police of an eighteen-year-old cantor, the young student Grzegorz Przemyk, for whom he had high esteem. Jerzy let loose during the Mass for the fatherland in May 1983. "Satan dared to perpetrate such a

---

[4] Popiełuszko, *Carnets intimes*, 31.

[5] "Meditation on the Way of the Cross" during a workers' pilgrimage to the Shrine of Częstochowa on September 28, 1983, in ibid., 60.

[6] Ibid., 63.

horrible crime that all Warsaw is mute with fear. He broke the thread of an innocent young life. In a brutal way, he deprived a mother of her only son."[7]

The priest set up a cross in the garden of the parish church in his memory. (I have had the grace of meditating there several times. In a bitterly ironic turn of events, he himself rests today in the shadow of that memorial cross.) Jerzy was crushed by that tragedy. For the first time he realized that death was no longer a vague threat, that a similar fate awaited him. It was a profound shock. Anguish seized him. On the photos from that period he appears thinner, with a preoccupied expression and drawn features that betray deep interior torments.

In that gloomy climate, the Holy Father's airplane landed in Warsaw on June 16, 1983. Officially, this second visit of the pope on his native soil was for the purpose of celebrating the six hundredth anniversary of the Shrine of Częstochowa. But obviously it was not devoid of political ulterior motives. John Paul II knew that Polish society, weary of fighting, was tempted to lower the flag. He secretly hoped that this journey would inspire a general resurgence and revive the hope of the nation. In order to put a spoke in his wheels, the Communist government forbade him access to Gdańsk, where most of the leaders of Solidarność were still languishing in prison. The Holy Father took the hit but prepared his response. Keeping a low profile or mincing his words was now out of the question. At Saint John Cathedral in Warsaw, he mentioned "the bitterness of disappointment, of humiliation, of suffering, of the loss of the freedom, and of human

---

[7] Homily at a Mass for the fatherland, May 1983, in Popiełuszko, *Chemin de ma croix*, 121.

dignity being trampled underfoot".[8] Several days later, in Częstochowa, where banners with the Solidarność logo managed to get past the checkpoints of the security services, he proclaimed the lament of a whole population: "I want to stand before the Mother of God," he said, "I want to bring her all the sufferings of my nation, and at the same time its desire for victory that does not abandon it."[9] The ovation that he received was extraordinary. The pope offered balm to the hearts of the Poles, revived their courage, reawakened their confidence. Father Jerzy, who was in charge of the medical service as in 1979, remembers the incredible success of that journey. In one homily he marveled: "Despite the pitch-black night in which we were plunged, despite the fading hopes, despite our sufferings, a ray of God's grace shone on our fatherland: the visit of our Holy Father John Paul II. Let us thank the Lord for having strengthened us, through him, in the assurance that we are on the right track."[10]

This papal visit did an awesome amount of good to Father Jerzy, too. "This pilgrimage, which was an extraordinary national, religious, and patriotic plebiscite, has strengthened me in my work and confirmed the validity of its approach."[11] The priest felt reassured also by the many postcards that he received then from all over Poland—"words full of warmth that I do not deserve", he said modestly—in thanksgiving for the hope and courage that he gave with the Masses for the fatherland, the impact of which had never been so strong. His popularity

---

[8] John Paul II, Homily for the Mass at Holy Cross Cathedral in Warsaw, June 16, 1983.

[9] John Paul II, Allocution in Jasna Góra, June 19, 1983.

[10] Homily at a Mass for the fatherland, June 1983, in Popiełuszko, *Chemin de ma croix*, 128.

[11] Popiełuszko, *Carnets intimes*, 35.

soared at that time to dizzying heights. In June 1983 he wrote in his journal: "It is becoming difficult for me to appear in public. Right away there are ovations: I have to autograph books and pictures. I would like to be alone, to be able to work in recollection, but now it is a steady grind from morning to evening."[12]

It was all very well for him to complain, to dream of anonymity; those signs of support and affection reinforced him in his commitments. "I am convinced that what I am doing is just and good", he confided to those closest to him. And even the pressures from the government, which plunged him into the depths of anguish, served as an encouragement. The police regime was expending an enormous amount of energy to silence him; was this not the best proof that his battles were for a just cause? Was it not an implicit admission that Christ was a threat to its power and that the Gospel was a liberating power that had to be contained, whatever the cost?

Fatigued, therefore, but confirmed in his desire to resist, the priest again took up his pilgrim's staff. On August 30, he traveled to Gdynia to give a retreat to the Sisters of Loreto. Police cars tailed him from Warsaw and parked in the convent courtyard throughout his stay. Jerzy was almost a nervous wreck. This lead weight was suffocating him—even more so because the regime then expanded its oppressive toolkit by resorting to judicial proceedings. On September 23, the regional district attorney's office began an investigation: the priest was accused of misusing his freedom of conscience and of worship, of being "detrimental to the interests of the people's Poland". Several weeks later, he learned that he appeared on the list of the "sixty-nine extremist priests" drawn up by the Jaruzelski government, which was also orchestrating a violent media campaign to portray him as "a political fanatic, an agitator, and a hothead" whose Masses resembled "hate meetings" and "political rage sessions". Jerzy, who had increasingly dark circles under his eyes, said in his own defense: "Proclaiming the word of God is not engaging in politics, although the Church has the right to intervene in the political domain every time the latter acts against divine or human laws. No one can prevent a priest from proclaiming the truth. I am not engaging in politics; I am a simple witness of Jesus Christ, a witness to truth, justice, and freedom."[13]

Jerzy had no bitterness or resentment toward his "executioners". "I do not even feel anger toward them, but only something like a strange uneasiness: How is that possible in the same fatherland? Are these men still Poles? Can anyone sell himself like that?"[14]

Despite the torments that were inflicted on him and the humiliations to which he was subjected, there was no hatred in him. "Glory to those who suffer for the fatherland, who do not bend under the yoke of the police methods",[15] he wrote simply. The wellsprings of his influence and heroism are here, in this supernatural ability to dam up hatred, to resist violence, and to turn the other cheek. He said in his sermons:

> Violent force cannot conquer, even though it may triumph for a time. We have the best example of this at the foot of Christ's Cross. Here, too, there was constraint and hatred of the truth. But violence and hatred were conquered by the Lord's love. Let us therefore be powerful in

[13] Homily at a Mass for the fatherland, July 1984, in Popiełuszko, *Chemin de ma croix*, 187.

[14] Popiełuszko, *Carnets intimes*, 48.

[15] Ibid., 15.

love, by praying for our brothers who have gone astray, without condemning anyone, but while unmasking evil. We will go to the resurrection, to victory, through the cross; there is no other path.[16]

Meanwhile the pressure from the police and the courts became more pronounced. On December 12, 1983, summoned by the prosecutor, Jerzy went to police headquarters escorted by his two lawyers, Edward Wende and Tadeusz de Virion. For long hours they verified his identity, how he spent his time, his associations. He was then taken to his apartment to conduct, they told him, a routine search. As he calmly entered his residence with a clear conscience, convinced that the services would find nothing compromising, Jerzy did not suspect that he had just sprung a trap. In a scenario of diabolic subtlety, during the interrogation the police had made use of the time to interfere in the apartment and to plant evidence to prove the charges. It was a full-scale operation. The priest recalls: "There were more than 15,000 copies of illegal writings, leaflets from Solidarność, the forbidden labor union, a coded document in French, thirty-six pistol cartridges, some plastic explosive, some dynamite with a detonator, four tear-gas grenades and five tubes of printer's ink."[17] The authorities intended to portray him as a terrorist in the pay of foreign powers.

It was such a huge trove that Jerzy's first impulse was to joke about it: "The Lord gave me the strength to look at all that calmly. I began to laugh, saying, 'Gentlemen, you exaggerate. . . .'"[18] But there was nothing funny about what happened next. After a sham trial, and despite his

---

[16] Homily at a Mass for the fatherland, March 1983, in Popiełuszko, *Chemin de ma croix*, 102.

[17] Popiełuszko, *Carnets intimes*, 39.

[18] Ibid.

vehement denials, Jerzy underwent the humiliation of being stripped naked for a complete search, and then he was thrown into a cell where other detainees awaited him. "One was suspected of having killed his wife and thrown her into the Vistula River; another of having participated in an assassination; still another of being responsible for the death of four persons. . . . They gave me a mattress, a light blanket and I stretched out on the ground. My cellmates behaved benevolently toward me."

So the assistant priest advanced a step farther in his Passion. Indeed, we cannot help thinking about Christ here, the innocent man considered to be a common criminal. Secret negotiations between the government and the primate, Cardinal Glemp, nevertheless led to the rapid release of the priest, who was crowned with new battlefield glory. Jerzy recalls: "The news was so important that radio and television reporters were waiting for me at the exit. I went right away to Saint Stanisław church, where in my honor there was a large cross made of candles, topped with the "V" of victory. A crowd stood in front of the rectory, and at the window was Father Bogucki, who waved to me, tears in his eyes. My room was full of flowers."[19]

Shortly after his release, Father Popiełuszko received a summons issued personally by the primate, Józef Glemp. Jerzy went to the chancery reluctantly. He knew that he was not viewed kindly by the cardinal archbishop's entourage, that many of his counselors thought that he was going too far, that his runaway fame—his homilies were now broadcast by free radio stations outside the country—was arousing jealousy, and that he did not have

[19] Ibid., 42.

a place in the primate's heart, either. It must be said that the latter was in a delicate situation. As a man of compromise, the defender of a conciliatory position with regard to the Communists who was concerned about avoiding a confrontation that could turn into a bloodbath, he was the object of constant pressure by the civil authorities. Now "the Popiełuszko case" was a thorn, a stumbling block in his relations with the regime. Henryk Wujec, a former officer of Solidarność, relates: "The authorities wanted to muzzle Jerzy. They harassed the primate so that he would stop his Masses and remove him from Saint Stanisłaus."

The meeting between the cardinal archbishop and his young priest was turbulent. Father Jerzy, who did not make a habit of pouring his heart out, says it with restraint in his personal journals: "The primate's rebukes overwhelmed me. The security services, during their interrogation, had respected me a lot more! That is not an accusation, but the expression of suffering. My God, to what trial are you subjecting me?" [20]

Essentially very little of their conversation became known except the invitation extended to Jerzy to stand back by going to Rome to study for a year or two. The young assistant pastor rejected this insistent proposal. He did not want to leave. In his mind it was impossible to let down the people, to abandon his parishioners, the families, the young people, the workers, especially those of the Huta Warszawa steelworks and the ties of their long companionship. His place was there, in the midst of the Poles who were his life, his family. "I was with them in the successful days; can I abandon them now that they

[20] Ibid., 43.

are being persecuted? Where will they go? They need help, I cannot refuse them", he confided to those closest to him. He then added: "Yes, I happen to be tired, and I do not have enough time to serve everybody. I am never free for myself, but I feel no discouragement. I will stand by the workers as long as I can."

For Father Jerzy, the year 1984 started under a bad omen. Ever since he had overturned the operation designed to put him behind bars, the police harbored a ferocious hatred of him. It had only one obsession: to reduce that troublemaker to silence. The threats, the intimidation aimed at those close to him, the searches, interrogations, court summons, and slander campaigns doubled in their intensity. Jerzy no longer had a normal life. The harassment reached the heights of cowardice. Father Czesław Banaszkiewicz, who recently came to visit me in Créteil with some relics of Jerzy, of whom he was a close friend, remembers that climate of terror. "He received a large number of anonymous threats. He was attacked in writing and by telephone, day and night: 'You will be crucified!' 'You will be hanged!' 'We will throw you from a train!' The police did not let him alone for an instant; he felt hunted down like a mad dog, persecuted, almost tortured."

During that period the priest was wrestling against fear, a fear that tormented him, although he did not want to succumb to it. His homilies are full of exhortations to block the path of that feeling. "Fear is the greatest failing of an apostle; it restricts the heart and contracts the throat. Someone who remains silent about the enemies of the good cause emboldens them."[21]

---

[21] Homily at a Mass for the fatherland, October 1982, in Popiełuszko, *Chemin de ma croix*, 58.

In another passage from a sermon, we get the impression that he is trying to convince himself: "Have no fear of those who kill the body; they can do nothing else. Remember that the Christian should be afraid only of betraying Christ for a bit of tranquility."[22]

Truly, you could tell that the priest was paralyzed. He gave the impression of being alone, terrified, facing a horde of enemies against whom he was waging a fierce battle. Death, which long ago had ceased to be an abstract hypothesis, now inhabited every one of his thoughts and prowled around him like a vulture over his prey. Jerzy was forever on the alert.

The months of January and February 1984 were a very trying period in his life, but also a very productive one. During that handful of weeks, what was without a doubt the most decisive stage of his whole spiritual life played out. Jerzy experienced then in his flesh the ordeal of Jesus in the Garden of Olives: that moment of extreme solitude and tension when the Son of man begged his Father to save him from death, to spare him the suffering of the Cross. "Being in an agony he prayed more earnestly; and his sweat became like great drops of blood falling down upon the ground", the evangelist Luke writes. Peace of mind finally came when Christ, after an intense interior struggle, agreed to leave it up to God, in other words, to die to his desire, to his will, to himself. This was the battle that was being waged in the soul of Jerzy, who was still unable to utter the sentence spoken by Jesus to his Father: "Not my will, but yours, be done."[23] Father Popiełuszko was not ready for this abandonment, this handing over of himself. He was on the brink of consent

---

[22] Jerzy Popiełuszko, *Méditations du chapelet* (Bydgoszcz, October 19, 1984). See appendix.

[23] Luke 22:42.

but did not yet have the interior freedom, the detachment that would allow him to say, like Saint Paul, "I do not account my life of any value",[24] or like Charles de Foucauld: "I abandon myself to you; do with me as you please."

A religious friend of Jerzy, the Ursuline nun Jana Płaska, remembers a meeting with him in January 1984: "He was sitting in front of me, near my desk, and he said to me: 'I have no strength left, physical, psychological, or spiritual.'" To bring him out of that dejection, she suggested that he get away for several days in an Ursuline convent in the mountains, near Zakopane. Overwhelmed with exhaustion and tension, Jerzy accepted. He spent about ten days there. Days of solitude, silence, and retreat. Aside from the Masses that he celebrated with them every day, the sisters saw little of him. He returned late from his long solitary walks and spent hours in uninterrupted prayer. He wrote in his journal:

> Today, before lunch, I went to the choir of the church to say my Rosary. A blessed silence. On the ambo was a gilded cross. From time to time a ray of sunlight got through, and the cross was illuminated as though it were made of gold. A divine warmth. Then dusk fell. My God, how that resembles everyday life: grey, heavy life, occasionally dismal and often even unbearable. Fortunately there are rays of joy, of your presence, a sign that you are there, in the midst of us, always the same, good, and merciful.[25]

What happened, then, during those days of retreat? What was the content of his prayer? On which of his

[24] Acts 20:24.
[25] Popiełuszko, *Carnets intimes*, 44.

heartstrings did the Lord play? Was the fact that he prayed the Rosary his main interior support during those diffi-cult times? Should we see in it the intercession of Mary, whom Father Popiełuszko loved madly, like every self-respecting Pole? While meditating on the Blessed Virgin did he understand that the spiritual life is nothing other than consenting to the will of God, accepting what hap-pens, saying "yes, so be it"? The fact remains that he returned from his retreat transformed. "There my spiri-tual rebirth began", he jotted in his journal. The prayer of hearts that are sorely tried is always productive, and I believe that Jerzy obtained from God there the grace of abandonment. A sort of reluctance was cleared away, something was untied. At the conclusion of a brutal strug-gle, he agreed to lay down his arms and to hand the reins over to the Lord. Then the anguish that gnawed at his heart disappeared, and this confident abandonment gave him wings. The photos from that time tell in their own way the story of this tipping point: in them Jerzy seems liberated, light-hearted, cheerful, unselfconscious. The torments that had darkened his face a few weeks earlier gave way to big smiles, a form of unclenching. Love, that is, free consent to the gift of self, drove out fear. Jerzy no longer belonged to himself; he was entirely commended into God's hands, ready for anything, even death.

For those around him, this change was edifying. This young, thirty-seven-year-old assistant priest now radiated assurance, serenity, a calm strength. In his prayer there was now a combative stubbornness that gave him tremen-dous courage. Father Józef Maj, his seminary classmate, writes: "There is no doubt that in the last year of his life, as he was led by the Lord, Jerzy matured at a faster rate.

I remember very well observing in him an increase in the concentration and intensity of his prayer and a growing awareness of his responsibilities."

Capuchin Father Gabriel Bartoszewski, who today is the promoter of the cause of his canonization, was struck, too, by these changes, especially at a meeting during the summer of 1984:

> We mentioned the possibility of him receiving a different pastoral assignment. Then, after a brief reflection, he uttered this decisive, poignant sentence: "I have dedicated myself, and I will not withdraw." Then a very long silence set in among us. His face, still calm and serene, had darkened momentarily. The words that he had uttered expressed profound determination. Personally, I felt something like an intense shudder. This event is engraved on my memory, and the recollection of that shudder is still with me.

Jerzy knew that the Holy Father supported him, and that made him all the more inflexible, determined to sacrifice himself for God and for his brethren. The pope had recently sent him a rosary and this word of support: "Be strong!"

During the months that followed, the priest was arrested thirteen times by the police. He wrote: "Genuine oppression, but Almighty God gives me spiritual fortitude. Psychologically I feel well. I no longer am afraid, I am ready for anything. The people are wonderful. Always flowers, always letters of solidarity."[26]

Now he preached wherever they invited him: in Gdańsk, in Częstochowa, and in many other cities in Poland. On October 13, while returning from the Baltic, and thanks

[26] Ibid., 48.

to his driver's virtuosity, he miraculously escaped an accident staged by the police: huge stones thrown onto the windshield. Jerzy then took seriously the imminence of his death, signed a Last Will and paid a visit to his parents. "Is it not preferable to die than to allow the lack of integrity to proliferate?" he told them to console them.

In his sermons, Father Popiełuszko invited young Poles to meditate on the eagles that appear on the national flag.

> You must fortify your soul and raise it very high so as to be able to fly above everything, like them. Only by resembling eagles will you brave the winds, the storms, and the tempests of history, without allowing yourselves to be enslaved to falsehood. The duty of a priest is to speak the truth, to suffer for the truth, and, if he must, to give his life for the truth. Let us pray that our whole life may be permeated with truth.[27]

Nothing seemed to be able to stop the free speech of that priest. Jerzy was a troublemaker who had to be eliminated.

---

[27] Homily at a Mass for the fatherland, February 1984, in Popiełuszko, *Chemin de ma croix*, 173.

6

The Way of the Cross

Have mercy on me, O God, for
men trample upon me; all day long
foes oppress me. . . . In God I
trust without a fear. What can flesh
do to me?

—Psalm 56:1-5

When he climbed into the front seat of his Volkswagen on Friday morning, October 19, 1984, Jerzy was not at his best. Feverish and aching all over, he was getting over a bad cold, and his face, darkened by large black circles under his eyes, still showed signs of fatigue. No doubt he would rather have stayed in bed instead of venturing onto the roads. But he was a man of his word: he had promised Father Osinski that he would come to say Mass and recite the Rosary in his parish in Bydgoszcz, northwest of Warsaw. For several months, invitations to preach had come in from every corner of Poland. Jerzy, who did not belong to himself anymore, made sure to accept them all. His presence, they said, did the people good. It was a balm that gave them consolation, courage, and faith in the future. Despite his illness and the icy cold of that autumn day, there he was sitting in his Golf, which was eating up the 190 miles between Bydgoszcz and the capital.

As soon as they left Warsaw, his faithful driver, Walde-mar Chrostowski, spotted a car following them; he could make out the presence of three men inside it. With an undeniable sense of prudence, he memorized the make, a Polski Fiat 125P, and noted the license plate number. The car tailed them as far as Bydgoszcz and parked not far from the parish of the holy Polish martyrs, where Father Popiełuszko was welcomed in the early afternoon by the pastor, Father Osinski. Warned about that suspicious presence, the latter dissuaded Jerzy from preaching at the 6:00 P.M. Mass, but kept his recitation of the Rosary on the schedule: alone at the altar, he would be too easy a target, whereas, while reciting the Rosary, he would be submerged in the midst of the crowd and the other priests!

It was seven o'clock in the evening. The Mass had just ended; the church was bursting at the seams. A solemn silence fell on the crowd in attendance when Jerzy appeared. In a faint, sick voice, the priest started the prayer with an invocation to the Blessed Virgin: "Mary, Mother of the land of the Poles, you are our hope; we kneel before you. Today we wish to take up our cross, the cross of our work, our sorrows, our problems, and to follow the way of your son to his Calvary and his agony."[1]

Suffering from a fever, with his legs unsteady and his forehead beaded with sweat, Jerzy stood firm thanks to the fervor of the faithful, which seemed to double with each Hail Mary. His meditation on the Sorrowful Mysteries displayed the major themes of his teaching: spiritual resistance to everything that tramples on the dignity of the human being, the sacredness of conscience, man's aspiration to truth, freedom, and justice, the call to overcome

---

[1] Jerzy Popiełuszko, *Méditations du chapelet* (Bydgoszcz, October 19, 1984). See appendix.

fear, the invitation to stay calm and self-controlled, since "only someone who has failed to win hearts and minds tries to prevail by violence, which is always an admission of weakness." At the back of the church one man furiously stamped his feet, as though each word caused a stabbing pain. His face was distorted with hatred. Jerzy recognized him as one of the men in the Fiat that morning. After an hour and a half, it was time to conclude the prayer. "Let us pray that we may be freed from fear and intimidation, but above all from the desire for revenge and violence." [2] These were his last words uttered in public.

When the prayer service was over, Father Osinski insisted that the guest priest stay overnight at his rectory, but Jerzy turned down his offer. He intended to return to Warsaw during the night so as to celebrate the nine o'clock morning Mass at Saint Stanisław, as he had promised. At 9:00 P.M., after a short dinner and the customary farewells, his automobile disappeared into the night. Jerzy asked Waldemar to observe the speed limits so as not to tempt fate. Nevertheless, as soon as they left the urban area, a vehicle started to follow them, tailgating them and incessantly flashing the high beams. Then it passed them and signaled for them to stop. Fearing the worst, the driver sped up, but Jerzy, who thought it was a simple routine inspection, told him to obey. Waldemar recalls: "He had no premonition of the danger, and he did not associate this inspection with the assassination attempt made on us the previous week, when a man had thrown stones against the windshield of our car as it traveled at a high speed on the road from Gdańsk to Warsaw."

The driver slowed down and parked the Golf on the

---

[2] Ibid.

shoulder somewhere between Bydgoszcz and Toruń, not far from the village of Przysiek, in the middle of a forest. The two vehicles turned off their motors. After a minute or two that seemed interminable, three men got out of the Polski Fiat. One of them, who was outfitted in a uniform, walked slowly to Jerzy's car and told the driver to get out to take a sobriety test: a mere formality, he said. The moment he stepped out, Chrostowski was grabbed around the waist by one of the policemen, who gagged and handcuffed him and locked him into the front seat of the Fiat, threatening him with death if he returned. Then everything sped up. With a revolver held to his temple, the driver could not see what was happening behind his back, but he heard the sounds of a struggle, violent blows, and Jerzy's voice exclaiming, "Officers, what are you doing? How can you treat me like this?" "Then I heard the sound of a trunk opening and a heavy weight being thrown in", Chrostowski continues, who guessed correctly: after being beaten on the back and the head, Father Jerzy, half conscious, had been thrown into the trunk of the Fiat, which zoomed off, leaving the Golf unoccupied on the shoulder. Resisting the intense urge to panic that seized him, the driver sketched a thousand scenarios. "First I thought of grabbing the steering wheel to make the car roll over, but then I realized that the priest would not survive it! At all costs I had to appear calm so as not to draw the attention of the attackers, but my mind was agitated, seeking a way to escape and to save Jerzy."

Finally, when the police car pulled out to overtake another in a well-lit urban area, Waldemar opened the passenger door while they were still passing and jumped from the traveling vehicle. During his fall the handcuffs gave way, but he was unhurt. Thus freed from his shackles, he went to alert trusted individuals. If it were not for that heroic act, we would know nothing about what happened!

News of the abduction blared the next day. Father Marcin Wójtowicz, one of the assistant pastors at Saint Stanisław, remembers:

> I was very surprised on Saturday morning not to see Jerzy at the Mass that he was supposed to celebrate at nine o'clock. That was not like him! At ten o'clock I finally received a telephone call informing me that he had been abducted the evening before. What a shock that was! Then the information was broadcast on television. Immediately afterward, people converged on the church. They were weeping, reciting the Rosary. The emotion was at a tremendous pitch.

Saint Stanisław Church remained filled with the crowd and the murmur of sobbing. The hope of regaining their assistant pastor was on the minds of the parishioners as they embraced one another and took turns keeping a prayer vigil night and day. Tokens of friendship and support poured in from all over the country. In Gdańsk, Father Jankowski, a friend of Jerzy's and chaplain of the Lenin construction sites, exclaimed, "Something unheard of in the history of Poland has happened, an act foreign to our people." Overwhelmed, Lech Wałęsa made the trip to Warsaw to comfort the laborers in the steelworks, who were lamenting their pastor, and to call them to remain calm and dignified. Almost everywhere in the country Masses were said for Jerzy's liberation. Within a few hours, all of Poland was on its knees.

On the 22nd, the Polish episcopate issued a press release: "The abduction of Father Popiełuszko causes the utmost anxiety. We fear for his life, and we fear also that kidnapping may become a weapon in the political struggle. The information that we have about the circumstances of his abduction leads us to think that the abductors acted for political motives."[3]

Under pressure from the popular sentiment that was spreading like wildfire, the authorities were in dire straits. Jerzy's driver had spoken and challenged the police: it was impossible to remain silent about the matter! This blunder could lead to insurrection; a response was necessary. On the 23rd, the government spokesman, Jerzy Urban, called a press conference: "All the police in the country are looking for the priest", he declared, embarrassed. The next day General Jaruzelski played the same transparency card: "Everything will be brought to light", he promised.

On October 24, in order to express his solidarity with the Polish people, Pope John Paul II put pressure on the government: "I share the justified concern of the population about this inhuman act that is an expression of violence committed against a priest and a violation of the dignity and inalienable rights of the human person."[4]

The next day it was the turn of the primate of Poland to tighten a little more the vice gripping the regime: "Having no news about Father Popiełuszko, we fear that Poland has become the scene of a murder similar to those endured by countries afflicted with the plague of terrorism. We demand that everything possible be done to shed light on the causes, the instigators, and the circumstances of this odious act."[5]

---

[3] Cited by Jean Offredo, "À Dieu Jerzy!", in Jerzy Popiełuszko, *Le Chemin de ma croix: Messes à Varsovie* (Paris: Cana, 1984), 3.

[4] John Paul II, Wednesday Audience, October 24, 1984.

[5] Cited by Offredo, "À Dieu Jerzy!", 3.

On October 27, the minister of the interior appeared in person on television on the 7:30 P.M. news. Visibly tense, General Kiszczak, a trusted deputy of Jaruzelski, revealed the names of the priest's attackers. They were three officials of his own ministry: Captain Grzegorz Piotrowski, thirty-three years old, head of the department of religions, and two of his lieutenants, Waldemar Chmielewski (twenty-nine) and Leszek Pękala (thirty-two). These henchmen acted under orders from Colonel Adam Pietruszka, vice-director of the department of religions and presumably the mastermind of the whole operation. For Jaruzelski's government, this revelation was a slap in the face, an admission that he did not control all his services, some of which, taking advantage of martial law, had set themselves up as fiefs directed by autonomous barons.

Based on Captain Piotrowski's confessions, searches were immediately undertaken in the region of Toruń. Hundreds of policemen were mobilized to comb the area. Finally, after three days of intense investigations, Jerzy's lifeless body was found in an artificial lake formed by the Włocławek Dam, several hundred miles from Warsaw. Father Feliks Folejewski was at Saint Stanisłaus Church when the guillotine blade fell:

> Right after Mass we announced Jerzy's death to the faithful. The first reaction was tears, outbursts of emotion, cries of sorrow that still reecho in my head. Then I went up to the microphone and started the prayer Our Father, which was immediately taken up by the crowd. I remember that we stumbled on the petition: "Forgive us our trespasses, as we forgive those who trespass against us." We needed to be disarmed, and so I asked the congregation to repeat that verse several times. But I sensed

the effort that it cost us. The parishioners were so angry that if I had said, "Let us go into the streets and break up everything", they would have run.

Henryk Wujec, a former Solidarność leader, confirms that when news of the assassination arrived, "we naturally thought of revenge, but then Jerzy's words calling us to overcome evil with good came to mind. If we resorted to violence, would it not contradict everything he had taught us and kill him a second time?"

In a message marked with great sadness, the Holy Father in turn exhorted the Poles not to let themselves be drawn into the spiral of hatred: "Let us pay our final respects to Father Popiełuszko in Christian dignity and peace. May the great significance of this death not be troubled or darkened in any way."[6]

On Friday, November 2, commissioned by Jerzy's parents to bring his body back to Warsaw, a small team traveled to the morgue in Białystok to which Jerzy's remains had been transferred. Father Grzegorz Kalwarczyk was one of them. He remembers the terrible moment when, escorted to the refrigerated room by the assistant attorney general, two physicians, and a colonel from the Ministry of the Interior, he opened a sealed door: "It opened onto a gurney on which lay the priest's naked body", he continued. "But Jerzy was unrecognizable." "If it had not been for the birthmark on his stomach, I would not have been able to recognize him; it was horrible", said Józef, Jerzy's young brother, who had come to identify him. Jacek Lipinski, a member of that same delegation, testifies:

[6] John Paul II, Wednesday Audience, October 31, 1984.

The only thing that I remember was my interior dread. At the sight of the countless mutilations, I said to myself: "My God, what did they do to you? They massacred you!" Had we not consulted his dental records, we could not have established his identity with certainty. I still see the crimson tint of his body, the alabaster white of his hands, the long wound that ran along his right arm and gave some idea of the violence of the blows he had endured. On his left leg the skin had been removed down to the flesh.

His disfigured face resembled that of Christ scourged and crucified, and his deformed mouth seemed to pronounce the words of the Suffering Servant: "I gave my back to those who struck me, and my cheeks to those who pulled out the beard; I hid not my face from shame and spitting" (Is 50:6).

They would have to wait for the trial in Toruń, in January–February 1985, to realize the full extent of the torment inflicted on Jerzy during the night of October 19. At the stand, the testimonies of his attackers, who were accused of premeditated crime, the intention to kill, and "acts of cruelty", would then make it possible to reconstruct the final hours of his life, during which Captain Grzegorz Piotrowski played the leading role. In court he would admit that he had acted for "political motives", thinking that the authorities "were fighting too half-heartedly against Popiełuszko's activities in support of Solidarność" and that "his department was not having enough success in its struggle against the anti-State activities of the priests."[7] This frustration, this per-

---

[7] "L'affaire Popiełuszko: début du procès" [Trial begins in Popiełuszko case], dispatch AFP/Reuter, December 27, 1984.

sonal hatred was what drove him to launch the puni-
tive operation, with the endorsement of his superiors.
During the trial, Piotrowski acknowledged that he had
beaten the priest "repeatedly" with "his fists and a spe-
cially made 21-inch nightstick". Jerzy's cassock, which is
preserved at Saint Stanisłaus parish, bears the marks of
rough fighting—proof that the priest tried to defend himself. But how could anyone resist when such violence was
unleashed, with relentless blows to the face? The nature
of his wounds, especially to his fingers, suggests that he
was tortured. No doubt the officials tried to extract from
him information about the clandestine structures of Solidarność, which he secretly attended. For two and a half
hours, in any case, Jerzy experienced a horrific Calvary.
At the conclusion, the policemen bound his hands and
legs and weighed down his feet with heavy stones. Then,
between pillars 4 and 5 of the bridge that overhangs the
Włocławek Dam, they threw his mutilated body like a
common carcass into the icy waters of the Vistula. It was
then 11:50 P.M. They did not know whether or not Jerzy
was still alive.

At the morgue in Białystok, the little team dispatched by
the family bustled about. While the men powdered the
face of the remains to give it a presentable appearance,
three Sisters of Charity proceeded to clothe it. Jerzy was
dressed in a white shirt, black slacks, and his cassock,
to which three insignia were pinned: one, against the
white and red background of the Polish flag, depicted
Our Lady of Częstochowa; the next bore the inscription "Solidarność, 1980–1984, Huta Warszawa" beneath
an eagle's head; and the last presented a view of Saint

Stanisłaus Kostka Church, captioned, "Masses for the fatherland, Warsaw". Over his cassock, the priest was covered with a red chasuble embroidered with ears of wheat and grapevine branches. A cross was placed in his hand, along with the rosary that he had received from John Paul II. Then the body was placed in an oak coffin and transported to a chapel, where the archbishop of Białystok, Edward Kisiel, sprinkled it with holy water and recited over it the final prayers. In one of the front rows, Father Kalwarczyk remembers next:

> Some priests then put the coffin on their shoulders to take it outside. Archbishop Kisiel walked at the head of the procession, wearing his episcopal vestments. Outdoors there was an immense crowd that was singing religious songs. Many of the faithful were holding funeral candles and tapers in their hands. Others took the coffin from the shoulders of the priests to carry it even higher. Many people were weeping. After making it through the crowd with difficulty, we placed the coffin and the sprays of flowers in the hearse.[8]

Then the convoy set out, laboriously clearing a path for itself through the streets that were black with humanity, where some of the Polish people waved lighted lanterns and others bid farewell in tears, while still others, running after the coffin, raised their hands making the "V" of victory. The priest continues:

> Hundreds of taxis and automobiles followed the hearse to the city limits. It was a concert of horns. The proces-

---

[8] Grzegorz Kalwarczyk, "Ce que j'ai vu à la morgue de Bialystok" [What I saw in the Białystok morgue], *L'événement du jeudi*, January 17, 1985; reprinted in Jerzy Popiełuszko, *Carnets intimes (1980–1984)* (Paris: Cana, 1988), 73–76.

sion moved slowly westward, so that the setting sun illumined the way. I will never forget that red sun. At the village of Żółtki, the limit of the Archdiocese of Białystok, the convoy stopped. Everyone got out of the cars to recite the Angelus with the inhabitants of the village who were waiting for us, kneeling on the roadway. Emotions were high. Even our driver was weeping.

Night began to fall when the convoy arrived in front of the door to Saint Stanisłaus Church in Warsaw. Tens of thousands of persons greeted Jerzy to the sound of bells tolling the death knell. The laborers from the Huta Warszawa steelworks were the ones who lifted the coffin onto their shoulders and carried it to the church, while the crowd repeated the song that had been sung so many times at Father Jerzy's Masses: "My Fatherland, so often bathed in blood, oh, how deep your wound is today, oh, how long your suffering lasts." At seven o'clock in the evening, a Mass was said in the presence of the body. Father Feliks Folejewski was one of the priests who concelebrated it. He recalls: "After the Our Father, I once more asked the faithful to repeat this verse: 'As we forgive those who trespass against us'. That was when I noticed Jerzy's mother, kneeling in the first rows. Clutching in her hand the cross and the rosary, she turned around toward the people and said, 'I forgive.' Even today I have difficulty holding back the tears when I recall that moment."

After the Mass and until dawn, the crowd filed past the open coffin and covered Jerzy with kisses and flowers. Then on Saturday morning, at 5:30, the church was closed to allow those closest to the priest a few moments alone with him. One could see his parents, Marianna and Władysław, his brothers and sister, a handful of priests, among them Teofil Bogucki, who loved him like a father, and several nuns. Bent over with grief, her hair covered with a black shawl, Jerzy's mother spoke: "It is very emotional for the others, but for the mother it is lifelong suffering! I do not wish on those who persecuted him that they should suffer as they made him suffer. May Jesus forgive them, may they be converted, and may they realize against whom they were fighting: not against my son, but against God! Now Jerzy is no doubt happy, but for us these are terrible days."

After the final farewells, the last touch of his cold hand, the coffin was closed, sealed, and then carried by the steelworkers and miners to a catafalque located outside, in front of the main doors of the church. The solemn funeral Mass began, with the primate of Poland presiding. Outside there was a sea of human beings. More than a half million Poles came to pay their homage to the martyr of their nation. Aside from the papal journeys, the country had never experienced such gatherings! All around the church, this impressively dignified crowd waved candles, flowers, crucifixes, and Solidarność banners. On some banners an inscription read: "Saint George, you will help us to defeat the red dragon", an allusion to the legend of the victorious battles of George—in Polish, Jerzy—against the monster, which is compared here to the Communist dictatorship.

Inside the church, Cardinal Glemp began his homily: "We believe that the sacrifice of the young priest's life will be the last on Polish soil and that no one else in our fatherland will make an attempt on the life of another man merely because he dislikes his teaching."

Physicians, artists, and laborers from the steelworks

spoke next. Then it was Lech Wałęsa's turn to offer a tribute in a voice choked with grief: "We bid you adieu, Servant of God, while promising not to bow to violence. In solidarity in the service of our country, we will respond to falsehood with truth and to evil with good. Recollected and with dignity we say farewell to you with the hope of a just social peace in our country. Rest in peace. Solidarność lives, because you gave your life for it."

At the moment when the coffin was being lowered into the ground, Father Teofil humbly stepped forward at the gravesite. In the midst of sobs and shouts, he declared that "The Polish ground has just received a new martyr." Then, speaking on behalf of an entire people, for whom there was no doubt about Jerzy's holiness, he added: "Only a great man, a saint, deserves a burial like this, with the participation of the cardinal primate, several bishops, and such a large crowd of the faithful. But we leave the decision to the sovereign will of God."

One day Jerzy had confided to a friend: "By his death and funeral, a priest can accomplish more than by his preaching." The Jaruzelski government, which indeed had anticipated that the priest would be more dangerous dead than alive, wanted to bury him as far away as possible, in Suchowola, for example, in the remote lands that saw his birth. But with the support of Jerzy's family and friends, the primate settled the matter and stood firm: he would be interred in Saint Stanisław churchyard, in that little plot of land that became, from the day of the burial, a place of pilgrimage where Poles come to renew their strength, courage, and hope. That crowd, united as a single man behind the tomb of this martyr, was a demonstration of strength against the regime. In his office, mentally reviewing Jerzy's statement over and over again, "You can crucify love and truth, but you cannot kill them",[9] General Jaruzelski understood that the crisis had reached a turning point. From now on it was impossible to resort to violence against this people, who could burst into flames at the slightest spark! The burial of Jerzy Popiełuszko definitively committed Poland to the path of dialogue.

[9] Homily at the Mass for the fatherland, March 1983, in Popiełuszko, *Chemin de ma croix*, 99.

7

The Martyr of Truth

He who does what is true comes to the light, that it may be clearly seen that his deeds have been wrought in God.

—John 3:21

On October 19, 2014, François, his wife, Chantal, and I landed in Warsaw, the capital of Poland, which was preparing to pay homage to Father Jerzy, thirty years to the day after his death. Several weeks after the opening of his canonization process in Thiais, in the Diocese of Créteil, this trip was a way of continuing the celebration with the Polish people and honoring with them the memory of the Blessed. For François, who had been preparing for it interiorly since his cure, this trip was also something of a pilgrimage to the sources, to the people, places, and scenes that had shaped the man to whom he owed his life. And so our hearts were pounding when our car drew up in front of Saint Stanisław Church.

In Warsaw, where we were received like royalty by the archbishop of the city, Cardinal Nycz, we made a series of visits, spurred on by the desire to survey all the places where Jerzy had left his mark, to meet the people close to him, to sense his presence. In the museum that occupies the basement of Saint Stanisław, we had the opportunity to handle the paten and the chalice with which he celebrated Mass and the torn cassock that he was wearing on the day of his abduction. This article of clothing has a gripping effect, and, in the presence of it, emotions run high. But they reached their climax in Jerzy's private apartment. Located on the second floor of the parish rectory, a few steps from the church, the place has not changed at all in thirty years. His former secretary and friend, Katarzyna Soborak, opened for us the room where everything still is now as it was then. The visitor gets the impression that Jerzy has just stepped out and his face will appear at any moment in the doorframe. Then, in the churchyard, we spent a long time in prayer at the foot of the priest's grave; I can still hear that profound silence resounding.

On October 18, after two days in Warsaw, we departed for Włocławek and the dam on the Vistula, where the priest had been thrown into the water after his long Calvary. From there, in the early afternoon, a long procession started out, preceded by relics of Jerzy. The crowd, which processed while meditating on the Rosary, was made up of delegations from Solidarność, local Christians, and regiments of albs and cassocks. Then an open air Mass was said at the place where a shrine dedicated to the priest will soon be constructed. François, Chantal, and I remained in the midst of those Poles, whose fervor gave me the chills.

The next day we returned to Warsaw, where another celebration was scheduled at Saint Stanisłaus. Two hours before the Requiem Mass, Jerzy's family was waiting patiently in a room at the parish center; they had asked to meet us. Present were Teresa, Jerzy's sister, his two brothers, Józef and Stanisław, and a host of nieces and nephews. We sensed quite vividly the priest's presence, if only in the facial features of his brothers, who strongly resemble him. Like old cousins who meet again, we spontaneously embraced each other. It was a very simple moment of communion yet full of warmth, emotion, and joy. The bell that sounded for the Mass at 5:00 P.M. interrupted that "family reunion", which would remain the key event of the trip. Covered with Polish flags, Solidarność banners, and portraits of the priest, the square in front of the church was packed with people. They came from all over Poland to salute the Blessed, the memory of whom is still very much alive. Then the Mass began. I was sitting in the first row of that church, which is very moving because it is still completely imbued with the priest's presence. After a moment, my attention drifted. I reviewed mentally the course of the last few days, punctuated by so many joys and intense meetings. While these memories were passing, I suddenly remembered a remark made by John Paul II after Jerzy's Calvary: "I pray that good may come of this death, like the Resurrection from the Cross. I still pray for that. May this death be the source of new life."[1] At that moment, a prayer of thanksgiving gushed from my heart, and at the same time I realized: Yes, the Holy Father's wish had been granted, a hundredfold even, since the death of Father Popiełuszko has produced an incalculable number of fruits!

The Church has known since the time of Tertullian that the blood of martyrs is a seed. It gives life, makes consciences fertile, and reveals the truth. In fact, Jerzy's sacrifice was a decisive step in Poland's long march for its liberation. First of all, it worked this first miracle: for the first time, the government of a totalitarian country of the Eastern Bloc was forced by public pressure to bring

---

[1] John Paul II, Audience with Polish visitors, November 5, 1984.

four of its security officers to justice. For two months, in January and February 1985, the debates unfolded in public, in front of the television cameras, amid popping flashbulbs and foreign correspondents. Even though it did not clear up all the mysteries, particularly the question of who silently approved of the assassination, no doubt some high-ranking official in the regime, the trial in Toruń revealed the responsibility and the methods of the Ministry of the Interior and made plain the hidden mechanisms of evil.

Having joined the procession of other Polish martyrs— Saints Adalbert, Stanisłaus, Andrew Bobola, Maximilian Kolbe . . . —Jerzy, like them, reminded his compatriots that it is possible to be faithful to one's conscience, to be a good human being, and to spread love during times of trouble, falsehood, and hatred. He hammered the point home during his lifetime: "A man who bears witness to the truth is a free man, even in external circumstances of slavery, even in a camp, even in a prison."[2] This message of refusal to submit galvanized the Poles. Conscious now of their strength and more certain than ever of the justice of their aspirations, even more people rose up to confront the regime. Indisputably, Jerzy's burial and the surge of resistance that it caused was a mighty blow of a battering ram against the wall of the dictatorship, which shook on its foundations. Faced with the people's determination, General Jaruzelski understood that he had no other choice but to engage in dialogue, without which a bloody insurrection would set fire to the country. With the arrival of Gorbachev at the head of the Communist Bloc and thanks

---

[2] Homily at the Mass for the fatherland, October 1982, in Jerzy Popiełuszko, *Le Chemin de ma croix: Messes à Varsovie* (Paris: Cana, 1984), 57.

to his policy of openness and change, called *perestroika*, Jaruzelski little by little loosened the vice that gripped the press, the intellectuals, the artists, the dissidents, and the religious in his police state. In January 1987, he traveled to the Vatican for a visit that was "historic", according to the pope himself. Under pressure from the Holy Father, with whom he developed the outline of a future "national reconciliation", the general yielded ground. In exchange for the diplomatic recognition of his regime, he promised to allow the beginnings of political pluralism and to include Polish society in discussions about the country's future. This resolution would take two years to become a reality: on February 6, 1989, broadcast all over the world, an absolutely unprecedented meeting in the East was called to order in Radziwiłł Palace in Warsaw, with the approval of Gorbachev at the Kremlin. Facing each other at the negotiating table were Lech Wałęsa, now finally recognized as the spokesman of the Polish opposition, and Jaruzelski's right-hand man, Kiszczak, the very same minister who had announced on television the arrest of Jerzy's murderers five years earlier. At stake in their discussions was the participation of Solidarność in a "national entente" to get the country out of its political, economic, and social rut. Is it necessary to recall that Jerzy was the first one to outline this solution of social dialogue and reconciliation, during the Mass for the fatherland in August 1984? He had prophesied: "The Polish nation harbors no hatred, and she is capable of forgiving much, but only at the price of a return to the truth. For the truth and the truth alone is the first condition for trust."[3]

After this meeting in February 1989, events followed

[3] Ibid., 194.

in quick succession. On April 17, the legalization of Solidarność was achieved. In June, great numbers of leaders of the labor union ran as candidates in elections for the legislature. It was an electoral triumph! On August 24, Tadeusz Mazowiecki, spokesman of Solidarność and a personal friend of John Paul II, was called on to form, for the first time in the history of Eastern Europe, a non-Communist government. Three months later, the Berlin Wall fell under pressure from the Germans and the winds of history. The collapse of that symbol of the ideological and political division during the Cold War prefigured the total dismantling of the Soviet Union that would take place in 1991.

Jerzy's sacrifice was therefore not a defeat. In throwing him into the water, his executioners thought that they were silencing him, but one cannot kill the truth. Underground, patiently, discreetly, it continues its work, harrows consciences, and ends up emerging into the daylight. With the other militants of Solidarność, whose devoted apostle he was, with the great anonymous crowd of dissidents, and supported by the activity of John Paul II, Jerzy helped to overturn Communism and its atheistic dictatorship of terror and falsehood.

Beyond these political and social advances there is another more intimate, more interior realm in which Jerzy's tragic death bore fruit: the hearts that were converted in great numbers to the Gospel through the intercession of his prayer. Like Pope John Paul II, who knelt at his grave on June 14, 1987, millions of people came to request a favor, to pray, to weep, to lay down their burden in front of Father Jerzy's modest marble tombstone, which is surrounded by evenly spaced stones connected by chains that trace the outline of Poland and symbolize the Communist oppression.

On the day of his burial, the rumor circulated that the regime intended to steal his body. A squad of workers therefore took turns watching over it. Today, the Communist threat is gone, but the tradition has been maintained. Wishing to stay in contact with the priest and never to leave him alone, they are on guard day and night, winter or summer, in snow or rain. There, over the course of thirty years, they have seen the most powerful individuals on the planet file past—the president of the United States, the prime minister of England, battalions of ambassadors . . . —but also major spiritual figures such as Mother Teresa and Brother Roger of Taizé, not to mention the pious crowd of anonymous souls who immediately discerned in Jerzy the mark of the great saints.

Since the day of the burial, the grave of the man whom John Paul II held up as "a model for the priests of the twenty-first century" has become a place of pilgrimage. For thirty years, flames have burned ceaselessly at its feet, and it has had a permanent covering of fresh flowers. They have lost count of the conversions that have occurred at this grave, which has also seen the birth of many priestly vocations. Father Tomasz Kaczmarek, the postulator of his cause of canonization, testifies: "Whether personal encounters with Christ, lights to discern a life-changing choice, help in various painful situations, or even healings, the many graces received from God through the intercession of Jerzy all have one thing in common: they always serve to revive the faith, to strengthen love of God, and to bring peace to the soul."

This shower of graces is the proof that Jerzy did not die in vain. Moreover, the Poles did not wait for the opening of his cause in 1997, or for his beatification in 2010, or even for the miraculous healing of François, to proclaim him a saint and to call for him to be raised to the honor of the altars. In their view, the Lord placed this dazzling figure on their path to convey to them this message: provided we allow God to do his work in us and remain faithful to the truth, to the voice of conscience, and to the willingness to sacrifice for love's sake, we can defeat the most terrible dragons and change the world . . .

Father Popiełuszko lived in the last century in a Poland that was affiliated with an empire that has broken up, under the pressure of an ideology that has been relegated today to the ash heaps of history. Does he still have something to say to us? Or does his spirituality of dissidence belong to a bygone era? Jerzy's case confirms that the saints never go out of fashion. Their message transcends the context that saw its birth, and the prophetic power of their insights is valid for all ages. Of course, in twenty-first-century France, priests are no longer imprisoned, the State no longer professes the Marxist-Leninist catechism, nor does it lapse into militant atheism. But the threats that weigh on the Christian faith and, therefore, upon man: Have they disappeared? Are they not even more insidious because they are more diffuse and less explicit? The combined attacks of secularism, dogmatic laicism, and rationalism promote the eclipse of God, do they not? Moreover, now that all limitations are commonly rejected, economic and social liberalism and its offshoots, hedonistic individualism, consumerism, and transhumanism reign unchallenged today—but are these ideologies capable of satisfying the profound aspirations of man? Surprised to learn that, after the cure of Sister Marie Simon-Pierre by

John Paul II, François is the second case of a miracle that has occurred in France through the intercession of a Pole, a high-ranking prelate in Warsaw told me one day in a humorous tone: "That is our fraternal way of giving you, our French cousins, a little lash of the whip, reminding you that the time has come to stand up and to take again your pilgrim's staff and to keep the promises of your baptism!"

I wonder whether this amusing observation deserves to be taken more seriously, along with the appeal made by Jerzy from his grave to oppose everything that stands in the way of faith and encounter with Christ, while never forgetting that the resistance to which the priest calls us is of a spiritual nature. It is a battle on our knees. We can conquer evil only through good, and the victory belongs to the one who loves—this is the message of the man who to the very end refused to sink into rancor and hatred. "Courage relies, not on the sword, but on the heart", he used to say. "Those who have not succeeded in conquering with the heart and the mind are the ones who strive to fight by means of violence."[4]

Unarmed, founded on prayer and forgiveness, the resistance promoted by Father Jerzy contains another original feature: it operates on the terrain of memory and nation. Condemned to death several times, Poland even disappeared from the map of the world and was subjected to Nazi barbarism and then a Communist dictatorship. If this great Slavic nation has survived its vicissitudes, Jerzy recalls, it has done so by remaining faithful to its culture, while cultivating its profound identity. Relying on the theology of the nation of John Paul II, he said: "Polish

[4] Ibid., 50.

culture is a treasure on which the spiritual good of the Polish people is founded. It defines us all through the history of our country more than material forces or political boundaries do. Thanks to its culture, our nation has remained itself, despite the loss of its independence for several years."[5]

In an era that promotes rootless individuals who are free of all attachment and cut off from the soil and their memories, this praise of the fatherland and of being part of a long history deserves to be pondered. The Blessed reminds us that a human person cannot be dignified if he is deprived of his identity, which sends down its roots into a particular geography, culture, and religion.

This is why Father Popiełuszko so ardently denounced those who tried to shelve his country's Christian past. In his view, to remove God from the life of the nation and to reject its Christian culture is to commit a twofold sin. First, against truth, because ever since its initial wedding with Christianity, this country has been shaped by the cross and the Gospel, like it or not. "You cannot create a history without a past and forget the Christian path of our nation, because a tree without roots topples over",[6] Jerzy used to say. But still more profoundly, to cut the nation off from its Catholic roots is to attack the dignity of the human person as such. "Man is really human only if he does not forget that he is a child of God",[7] Jerzy insisted; he advocated putting the Lord back at the heart of the political, social, and economic transformation of our coun-

---

[5] Ibid., 141.

[6] Ibid., 142.

[7] Jerzy Popiełuszko, "Meditation on the Way of the Cross" during a workers' pilgrimage to the Shrine of Częstochowa on September 28, 1983, in Jerzy Popiełuszko, *Carnets intimes: (1980–1984)* (Paris: Cana, 1988), 65.

tries and cultivating the spiritual dimension of our lives. This comes through, for example, in the priest's criticism of the Communist view of work, which tends to make man a mere beast of burden:

> The purpose of work is to serve man and to ennoble him. Matter cannot count more than the spiritual side. The man who works hard, without God, without prayer, without an ideal, will be like a bird with one wing, stuck on the ground. He will not be able to lift himself up and see the higher possibilities, the larger meaning of earthly existence. He will circle around his beak, like the injured bird.[8]

Justice therefore does not consist solely of liberating people from oppression and giving them a job and the means with which to live a decent life. Of course rights and material goods are necessary, but the human person is worthy of that title only when he can achieve his deeper vocation: to be united with God and to satisfy the desire for the infinite that dwells in his heart. This is why Father Popiełuszko defended so vigorously the sacredness of conscience, in the depths of which man discovers a small voice that is not his own, that calls him to love, to do good, and to live by God's life, in truth.

Truth. That is the word that best summarizes the life and teaching of Father Jerzy. The man who is often called "the martyr of truth" spent his life hunting down the lies of the Communists, and he revealed the thirst for truth that burns in the heart of every man. No, he whispers to us, all doctrines, all currents of thought are not

[8] Homily at the Mass for the fatherland, April 1983, in Popiełuszko, *Chemin de ma croix*, 108–9.

equally valid. We must not resign ourselves to relativism, "a dictatorship . . . that does not recognize anything as definitive and whose ultimate goal consists solely of one's own ego and desires", according to Benedict XVI. But if truth exists, and Jerzy believed that it does, what is it like, and where do we find it? Can one hold the truth without showing intolerance or pride? By the example of his life, Father Popiełuszko taught us that we are never the ones who possess the truth; rather, it possesses us. It is not a doctrine to be learned or defended but rather a living person: Christ, who comes to touch us, to capture us, and to shower us with his gifts so that we in turn might give ourselves. For truth is proved in love, in other words, in the gift of self for others. It engages the whole human being, when so many people live only superficially. It is demanding, it calls for sacrifices and self-denial, but, as Jerzy notes, is that not the price of true joy and freedom? He wrote:

> To preserve one's dignity as man is to remain interiorly free even in external slavery, to remain oneself in all situations of life, to remain in the truth, even if that is to cost us dearly. Because it costs a lot to speak the truth. Only the weeds, in other words, petty, mediocre things, are cheap. But for the wheat of truth, as with all great and beautiful things, one must pay the demanding price of self-sacrifice.[9]

---

[9] Ibid., 97.

God Works Miracles

*Jesus . . . went with them. But their
eyes were kept from recognizing him.*

—Luke 24:16

Almost four years have passed since Father Jerzy came into
my life and François was cured miraculously by his intercession. During that time I have often thought again about
all these events of which I have been the "eyewitness" (Lk
1:2). A historian of the mystical life wrote that a "miracle
is a proposal, an invitation to a personal change of scene".[1]
It makes no sense unless it inspires a conversion, a transformation of the person who sees it. How was my life renewed by this visitation by God?

In the first place, I received the grace of greater trust
and deeper prayer, which has caused me to take an addi-
tional step in self-abandonment. Not a day goes by without my saying to Jesus in our heart-to-heart conversation:
"I trust in you; do with me whatever you want!"

These events have also helped me to take a new look at
the daily routine. At first I wondered anxiously, "When
you have seen the heavens open, when God has shown
you his kingdom, how do you go back to a normal life?"

---

[1] Joachim Bouflet, *Une histoire des miracles du Moyen Âge à nos jours* (Paris:
Seuil, 2008), 36.

And then I understood this: the Lord is found nowhere else but in this everyday life. His glory is there, hidden in the little miracles of ordinary life—the expressive glance of a sick person whom I am visiting, the naïve question of a child in catechism class, the disarming smile from a woman passing by, the warmth of a handshake. . . . It is all about developing keener vision so as to spot this God of the little insignificant things and to marvel at him.

And then above all I grasped the fact that a miracle, understood as the sign of God's presence in our midst, is not an exceptional phenomenon. God unceasingly sends us these signs of his love and his salvation. In fact, there is a miracle at each step in our lives as believers. Only our preoccupation with seeing prodigies, our blindness, and our lack of faith prevent us from recognizing it.

The first time I became aware of this blindness was in 2004, during the night of anguish that precipitated my conversion.

That evening, upon returning from a business trip in Italy, I found my house entirely empty. Before running off, my second wife had taken everything out of it. Nothing was left, not one piece of furniture, not even a bed. Emptiness. I was desperate. Everything that I had built up—my marriage, a form of social success, certified by my house, my boat, my car . . . —collapsed like a sand castle. I see myself again alone in that big, cold house, telling myself: "Everything passes, everything is built on sand; yet is there anything stable on which to anchor one's life?" I did not sleep a wink that night. Prompted by an inspiration, I took a sheet of paper and jotted down everything I had experienced with my wife, for better or for worse. The more I conducted this internal review, the farther I was drawn back into the past. I went as far as my

Baptism, my childhood in Brittany swathed in the Christian religion, with its youth clubs, its catechism, and its scouting program. And I discovered then that in deserting the Church for forty years I had forgotten the essential thing: the Lord, who was the mainspring of my existence, its center and support. I was angry at him. Why had he waited all this time to manifest himself to me? Why had he not given me a sign earlier? The answer came at dawn, after my whole life had passed before my eyes. It was crystal clear: God had not stopped calling to me or blessing me with his presence, but I had heard nothing and seen nothing, I did not want to know anything about it.

Yet he was there in the 1970s. At that time I was apparently fulfilled: a married man and father of two boys. I was successful at everything. Professionally, I had quickly climbed the ladder to become the director of sales for a large dairy products business. I was earning a lot of money; I was surrounded by friends. And yet, deep down inside, there was a great dryness. The apparent happiness masked open wounds, such as estrangement from my wife, whom I had married too young, at the age of twenty-one, while still immature. I had everything, but I vaguely felt that something essential was lacking. Could God have inspired this awareness even back then?

He was there, too, in 1990, at the death of my twenty-seven-year-old brother. He was my little brother; I had dandled him on my knees when he was a baby. On the night he died, I left the hospital and drove around for hours. I felt so alone. His passing brutally confronted me with the absurdity of life, with the emptiness of everything I had built up while running in all directions—my first marriage, which had failed, my social success, which did not make me happy. I was like a man who is out of breath and all at once feels the need to take a break, slow down, and breathe. Today I know that God was the one whispering to me that call to catch my breath. Carried away by anger, I had not heard him.

Then the Lord was at work in my meeting with the woman who was to become my second wife in 1999. The youthful romance I had experienced as a young soccer player had reappeared like a ghost from the past. She was a widow and still just as beautiful. We loved each other a lot. But little by little the symptoms of the mental illness that afflicted her, which I had underestimated, became more intense. She was prone to episodes of paranoia and to an obsessive jealousy that became a threat to our marriage. The sick leaves due to her repeated bouts of depression were followed by suicide attempts. I felt bereft and helpless. In order to save our marriage, I risked everything to save it all: we left Cholet, which we had made our home, to build a big, beautiful house in Les Sables-d'Olonne with a view of the sea. I also bought a boat so as to go sailing on weekends. We had everything we needed to be happy. But the problems got worse. Her paranoia became increasingly severe. She spent her time following me, even when I traveled abroad, tracking my smallest movements, examining every piece of my clothing. One day, as I returned from work, I noticed a big blaze in the garden: she was in the process of burning all her belongings. The situation became intolerable; her dementia drove her to frequent stays in psychiatric hospitals. Until that day in 2004 when, upon returning from Italy, I discovered that she was gone after emptying the house entirely. Then again, during that overwhelming night, no doubt the worst in my life, the

Lord manifested himself by calling attention to his presence in my memory. And by making me understand that although I had forgotten him, he had always remained faithful . . .

Starting with that realization, the miracles followed one after another. The scales had fallen from my eyes; I could now detect the traces of God's action in my life.

First there was the reunion with Jesus in a little seaside chapel. I had entered by chance, only to leave one hour later at peace, as I had never experienced peace before, my heart enlarged, with the certainty that happiness was life with God. There was also the meeting with Father Timothée, prior of a religious community, who introduced me to the Bible, the sacraments, the liturgy, and prayer. When you begin to welcome Christ in this way, everything is changed, everything is new, everything is possible. I had the impression that I was being carried in Jesus' arms, which the Little Flower likens to an elevator, because they are always outstretched and offered to us, and when you do throw yourself into them, you are propelled to fantastic heights . . .

And then one year later, in 2005, after a long time spent in adoration in that same seaside chapel, there was the call to the priesthood. After having spent forty years of my life looking for better work, a bigger house, a faster automobile, more and more respect, I understood that happiness does not consist in climbing the social ladder, but in descending. Jesus himself had taken that route toward littleness by becoming a servant, by washing the feet of his disciples. Like him, I wanted to be with people, to serve them, to give them my heart, my time, and to live out the beautiful spirituality of a diocesan priest, which consists of creating ties between God and a community and between the people themselves.

After this call to give myself to him, God took on the features of the priests who welcomed my vocation, listened to me, and accompanied me, without ever judging me. It still gives me the shivers when I think about my meeting with Michel Santier, then the Bishop of Luçon. After listening to my story, he put his hand on my shoulder and said to me: "Bernard, I accept you as you are!" But not everything was that rosy; that is the least that can be said. Often my path toward the priesthood took on the appearance of an obstacle course. I was treated with hostility by Pharisaical prelates who thought that I was an outsider, that my business background was a blot on my record, and that my past disqualified me forever. The attitude of these pastors, who look at the Church as a customs office and spend their time issuing condemnations, caused me a lot of suffering. With hindsight, I think that the Lord was with me in these oppositions. He gave me the strength to take rejections, judgments, and low blows and to continue on my path until ordination, on April 15, 2012, a certain Mercy Sunday . . . And then I saw him at work, too, several months after François' cure—the miracle that confirmed my vocation in the eyes of everyone—when some of those hostile priests came to me and humbly asked me for forgiveness.

As I review in my heart the course of my life, I am overcome with amazement. I am filled with gratitude for this meandering story made up of detours and falls and missed meetings, which demonstrates the mercy with which the

Lord lifts up those who have fallen! The Jesuit François Varillon wrote: "We should never imagine [God] otherwise than rushing with his arms stretched out toward us."[2] I am proof that God is this loving father, hastening to be reunited with the child who has gone away from him. At heart he is goodness, forgiveness, and tenderness. For forty years I abandoned his presence, but every day, without growing weary, he watched and hoped for my return. He made appeals to me, sent invitations and signs. And finally, when I returned, my heart heavy with fatigue, he threw himself into my arms to hug me.

Some Catholics have resigned themselves and declare that the age of miracles is over. Yet the miracles have not dried up, even if our faith has. By dint of looking for the extraordinary, prodigies, we no longer see all around us the countless little signs of the Lord's loving presence.

When you are attentive to these visits from God and learn to discern the signs of his passage in our lives, then you sense the need to become a sign yourself, just as the sick people cured by Jesus became witnesses to the people around them. Father Jerzy Popiełuszko was one of those witnesses who reveal the face of the true God, the God who is close and merciful, who gives life, his life, abundantly.

"You are the light of the world", Jesus told us (Mt 5:14). In each of us Christ has placed this light. It is the light of love, of truth. It illumines the night, dispels the shadows, warms hearts, and communicates hope. For millions of Poles led astray by the falsehoods of a totalitarian State,

---

[2] François Varillon, *Joy of Faith, Joy of Life: Lectures on the Essential Points of the Christian Faith*, ed. Bernard Housset, trans. Maurice Verrier (Sherbrooke, Quebec: Éditions Paulines, 1993), 174.

Father Jerzy was that brilliant light, that signpost, that beacon which shows the safe way that leads to God. It is up to us, too, like him, to make the miracle of this light shine in our families, among our friends, in our lives, and in our countries.

Appendix

Meditations on the Rosary by Father Jerzy Popiełuszko, at the Church of the Holy Polish Martyrs in Bydgoszcz, on October 19, 1984, the day of his assassination.

Mary, Mother of our Polish land, our hope, sorrowful Queen of Poland. As we pray the Rosary today, we place ourselves in your presence, we, the men of the working world and members of "the oasis of the domestic Church". We want to stay beside your Son at the hour of his agony, to look at his face; we want to take up our cross, the cross of our daily work, our troubles and problems, and to follow the way of Christ as far as Calvary.

Support us, Mary, for we are tormented by physical wounds and pains. So often we experience worry, confusion, and discouragement; support us morally, O Mary. We are humiliated, deprived of human rights and dignity; revive our courage and our perseverance. Show to us who are striving to renew the face of this earth in the spirit of the Gospel your maternal protection, O Mary. Extend your helping hand to us who, in sorrow and with difficulty, are fighting for truth, justice, love, peace, and freedom in our country.

The First Sorrowful Mystery: The Agony of Our Lord in the Garden of Olives

The Holy Father John Paul II addressed the Blessed Virgin at Jasna Góra on June 23, 1982, with this prayer: "I thank you, Mother, for all those who remain faithful to their conscience, who fight all alone against weakness and strengthen others in this fight. I thank you, Mother, for all those who do not let themselves be overcome by evil but overcome evil with good."

Only the person who can overcome evil remains rich in goodness himself. The person who cares about his development and is enriched by the values that make up the human dignity of the child of God. To increase good and overcome evil is to care about the dignity of the child of God, about his human dignity.

Life must be lived with dignity, because we only have one life. It is necessary to talk a lot about human dignity today in order to understand that man is worth more than anything that can exist on earth except God. He is worth more than the wisdom of the whole world.

Preserving one's dignity so as to be able to increase good and to overcome evil means staying free interiorly, even in conditions of external enslavement, remaining oneself in every situation in life. As children of God, we cannot be slaves. Our divine adoption entails the inheritance of freedom. Freedom is given to man, and truth is the first feature of humanity. It has been offered by God not only for ourselves but also for our brethren, and hence the duty to claim it where it is still unjustly limited. Yet freedom is not only the gift of God, it is also our duty for our whole life.

Let us pray to the Lord Jesus Christ that each day we may preserve the dignity of the child of God.

The Second Sorrowful Mystery: The Scourging of Jesus at the Pillar

Preserving dignity so as to be able to increase good and overcome evil means orienting one's life in terms of justice. Justice proceeds from truth and love. The more truth and love there is in man, the more justice there is in him. Justice must go hand in hand with love, because without love one cannot be fully just. Where love and good are lacking, their place is taken by hatred and violence. If we let ourselves be guided by hatred and violence, we cannot speak about justice. Because of this, the effects of injustice are felt very painfully, and this is seen in countries were "governing" is based no longer on the service of love but on violence and constraint.

It is important for a Christian to become aware of the fact that God himself is the source of justice. It is impossible to speak about justice where there is no place for God and his commandments, where the word "God" has been officially eliminated from the life of the fatherland. Let us be aware of the unlawfulness and prejudice that are inflicted on our Christian nation when it is made atheistic by law, when they destroy in the souls of the children the Christian values that their parents have instilled in them from the cradle, the values that have proved themselves over the course of our millennial history, then doing justice and demanding it is the duty of everyone without exception. For as an ancient thinker said: "The times are evil when justice drinks water [instead of wine]."

Let us pray that, in our everyday lives, we will be directed by justice.

The Third Sorrowful Mystery: The Crowning with Thorns

"To overcome evil with good" is to remain faithful to the truth. The truth is a very subtle faculty of our reason. The aspiration to the truth was inculcated in man by God, and, hence, in man there is a natural aspiration to truth and an aversion to falsehood. Truth, like justice, remains connected to love, and love costs something. True love is obliging, and therefore truth, too, has its price to pay. The truth always brings men together and unifies them. The greatness of truth frightens mean, scared men and unmasks their lies.

For centuries there has been an uninterrupted battle against truth. The truth, however, is immortal, whereas falsehood dies a quick death; hence, as the late primate Cardinal Wyszyński said: "The men who proclaim the truth do not have to be numerous. Christ chose a small number of them to proclaim the truth. Only falsehood needs a lot of words, because falsehood is detailed and perishable, it changes like the merchandise on the shelves. It always needs to be renewed, to have many henchmen who, according to a program, will have to learn it by heart today, tomorrow, a month from now; then there will be emergency instruction in another falsehood."

We must learn to discern between falsehood and truth. It is not easy in the age in which we live. It is not easy in an age when, as a contemporary poet puts it, "Never before have our backs been scourged so much with the whips of falsehood and hypocrisy." It is no longer easy today, when censorship crosses out the true words and the courageous thoughts and even the words of the Holy Father. The Christian's duty is to remain in the truth, even if it costs dearly. For truth is worth it; only junk is worthless; sometimes you pay very dearly for the grain of wheat of the truth.

The Fourth Sorrowful Mystery: The Carrying of the Cross

In order to overcome evil with good, one must care about the virtue of courage. The virtue of courage is the mastery of human weakness, especially of fear and terror. Have no fear of those who kill the body; they can do nothing else. Remember that the Christian should be afraid only of betraying Christ for a bit of tranquility.

The Christian must not be content with the condemnation of evil, falsehood, cowardice, hatred, servitude, and violence but must be himself a true witness, the spokesman and defender of justice, good, truth, freedom, and love. He must demand these values in himself and in others.

Only a courageous man is truly prudent and just, the Holy Father said. Cardinal Wyszyński used to say: Woe to the society whose citizens do not conduct themselves with courage, because they cease to be citizens and become slaves. When a citizen gives up the virtue of courage, he becomes a slave and causes the greatest harm to himself, to his human personality, to his family, to his professional group, to his nation, to his State, and to the Church. It would be easy to enslave him by fear and anxiety for a little bit of bread or a few secondary advantages, but woe also to the leaders who try to capture a citizen at the price of intimidation and fear of enslavement. If the State governs frightened citizens, then its authority is degraded, and the life of the nation, its cultural life, and the value of its professional life are impoverished. Courage, therefore, must be a major concern of the authorities as well as of the citizens.

Let us ask Christ, who carried the Cross, to show us, in our daily lives, courage in the fight for truly Christian values.

The Fifth Sorrowful Mystery: The Crucifixion

In order to overcome evil with good and safeguard human dignity, we must not resort to violence. The Holy Father, during the state of siege, said in his prayer to the Madonna on Jasna Góra that the nation could not develop normally when it was deprived of the rights that condition its judgment. The State cannot be strong with the strength of any violence. Someone who has failed to win hearts and minds tries to prevail by violence. Every manifestation of violence is proof of moral inferiority. The most important and most consequential battles known to history have been the battles of human thought. The most miserable and the shortest have been the battles of violence. An idea that needs weapons in order to exist dies of itself. And idea that is nourished on violence alone is depraved. And idea that is capable of living conquers by itself and attracts millions of persons who follow it spontaneously.

The reason why Solidarność conquered the world so quickly is that it did not fight with violence but on its knees, with its rosary beads in hand. In front of the outdoor altars, it demanded the dignity of human work, human dignity, and respect for man. In the last year of his life, Cardinal Wyszyński said that in recent decades the world of laborers had experienced many disappointments and restrictions. Working men and all of society in Poland experienced the torment of the lack of fundamental rights of the human person, limitations on freedom of thought, restrictions on opinions about life, on the profession of faith in God, and on the education of the younger generations. All these things were stifled. When this oppression wearied the whole population intolerably, they rose up in a surge of freedom, and Solidarność appeared, which proved that one did not have to break with God in order to rebuild society and the economy.

Let us pray that we may be freed from fear and intimidation, but above all from the desire for revenge and violence.